Des *nline*

Design and Launch an Online

Travel Business

in a WEEK

◆ *Turn-key Solutions*

◆ *Situational Tips from the Experts*

◆ *Programming and Design Knowledge
Not Required*

Entrepreneur Press & Charlene Davis

**EP
Entrepreneur.
Press**

Jere L. Calmes, Publisher
Cover Design: Desktop Miracles
Production and Composition: Eliot House Productions

This publication is designed to provide accurate and authoritative information in regard
to the subject matter covered. It is sold with the understanding that the publisher is not
engaged in rendering legal, accounting or other professional services. If legal advice or
other expert assistance is required, the services of a competent professional person
should be sought.

Computer icon ©Skocko
Hand icon ©newyear2008

Library of Congress Cataloging-in-Publication Data
    Davis, Charlene, 1957–.
    Design and launch an travel business in a week/by Entrepreneur Press and Charlene
Davis.
       p. cm. -- (Click start series)
     ISBN-13: 978-1-59918-267-4 (alk. paper)
     ISBN 1-59918-267-X (alk. paper)
     1. Travel agents. 2. Travel—Computer network resources. 3. New business enter-
prises—Management. 4. Small business—Management. I. Title.
     G154.D384 2009
     910.68'1—dc22   2009000056

Printed in Canada

14 13 12 11 10 09   10 9 8 7 6 5 4 3 2 1

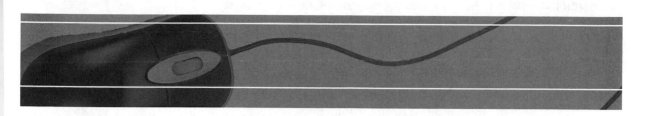

Contents

Acknowledgments

A number of people contributed to the success of this book, so I would like to take this opportunity to acknowledge and thank them for their wonderful insight, words of wisdom, and all-around great advice: Beth Whitman, Wanderlust and Lipstick; Dane Steele Green, Steele Luxury Travel; Sue Freeman, New York Outdoors; James and Heather Hills, Man Tripping and Chick Vacations; Chris Lopinto, Expert Flyer;

Dan Parlow, My Trip Journal; Jenny Reed, Our Cruise Planner; Jennifer Sage, Viva Travels; Al DiGuido, Zeta Interactive; Peter Geisheker, The Geisheker Group Inc.; Andi McClure-Mysza, Montrose Travel; Karen Hawkins, Off The Wall Emporium; and George Simpson, George H. Simpson Communications.

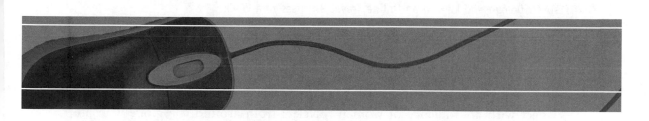

Foreword
by Beth Whitman,
wanderlustandlipstick.com

*A*s a passionate traveler for more than 20 years, I've done many things to reach out to the women's travel market in order to inspire and encourage other women to follow their dream journeys. This has included writing travel articles for print publications and teaching workshops in the Seattle area.

Initially, my reach was limited to my immediate community in the Pacific Northwest and those who happened to read my travel articles that appeared in newspapers and magazines across the United States. Until I launched my website, that is.

With an online presence at www.WanderlustAndLipstick.com, I now connect with an audience of women travelers from around the globe who are eager to learn how to make their travels safer, less expensive, and more interesting. I now have the ability to reach women in Western Australia just as easily as I can those in Western Washington. They come to my site looking for ethnic recipes, music reviews, and product recommendations. They subscribe to my e-newsletter, visit my website, and receive RSS feeds of my blogs.

In addition to providing a place for a growing community to share their travel information, I have also created a business that incrementally grows monthly through affiliate programs, ads, and sales of my books.

How does this help you? Consider the fact that you're already passionate about travel. Why not turn that enthusiasm into cash? With consistent dedication and enthusiasm, you, too, can create an income stream that will help you fuel your travels with the help of this new book from Entrepreneur's Click Start series: *Design and Launch an Online Travel Business in a Week.*

This comprehensive resource from Entrepreneur Press will help you arrive at your online destination by providing the key steps to developing, designing, and marketing your own travel website. You'll learn from the successes and failures of the many entrepreneurs interviewed for this book, and you'll be inspired to begin immediately.

You'll soon discover that your audience is but a few keystrokes away, ready to learn about your services, purchase your products, and subscribe to your newsletter.

Travel well,
Beth Whitman
wanderlustandlipstick.com

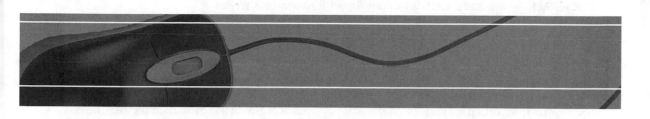

Preface

*I*t has never been easier than now to turn a passion for traveling into a lucrative, professional business. Travel and tourism constitutes the third largest retail industry in the United States, according to a study published by the Travel Industry Association (TIA). Only automotive dealers and food stores generate more revenue among retailers than the $650 billion travel and tourism industry. On average, travelers in the United

States spend $68 million an hour, or $1.6 billion a day. The time has come for you to tap into this quickly growing market that is embracing online travel.

There are, however, a number of responsibilities involved in running an online venture, just as there is with operating a brick and mortar business. The purpose of this book is to help you streamline those tasks so that your online business will run smoothly and efficiently. Plus I want to emphasize the importance of operating sensibly and ethically, while providing you with information and tools to assist in improving your performance as a professional travel specialist.

One of the neat things about running your own business is that you are the boss (aka head honcho, top dog, big cheese). The good news is that you get to make all of the decisions. The bad news is that you have to make all of the decisions. You also can't call in sick or defer someone to a higher authority. But don't worry, I'm going to help you get on top of your game with sage advice from successful travel entrepreneurs, strategies to market your business, nitty-gritty details about the travel industry, and much more.

This is a book for travel enthusiasts, but it's not about travel. It's about setting up and running an online travel business from anywhere in the world in just a few days. I'll provide you with the information you need to build and grow your business and get on the fast track to success. So relax, start reading, and explore all of the options that will show you how to become profitable in the travel industry.

Chapter 1

The Road Map
to Success

*M*any types of online businesses come and go in the blink of an eye. But the travel industry continues to grow by leaps and bounds, creating a big demand for specialized services. Statistics from the U.S. Bureau of Labor Statistics indicate that money spent on traveling will rise significantly over the next decade.

Worldwide, travel and tourism is an $8 trillion business, and in ten years that number will reach $15 trillion, according to the World Travel & Tourism Council (WTTC). The WTTC's long-term forecasts point to steady growth for world travel and tourism between 2009 and 2018, averaging 4.4 percent a year.

To help facilitate that growth, this book offers indispensable guidance by teaching travel enthusiasts how to set up an online travel business, create an attractive and functional website, learn the basic concepts of internet marketing, find qualified providers when outsourcing, automate their website to run smoothly in their absence, and take online payments while keeping track of the same, and what to do when things don't always go as planned. The best part is this exciting new business can be up and running by the end of the week!

Another great feature is the entrepreneur needs very little upfront cash to get started. Travel enthusiasts can turn a fun hobby into a lucrative business that can easily be operated at home on a shoestring budget. Because a degree or special certification is not required to get started, anyone—regardless of their current status—has the potential to successfully start an online travel business virtually overnight.

DON'T QUIT YOUR DAY JOB

Most of the travel entrepreneurs we interviewed advised against quitting a full-time job before you've had the opportunity to grow your online business. Many travel specialists start their businesses on a part-time basis and gradually evolve into a full-time operation. This allows for more flexibility, especially if you want to work around another job and keep that steady cash flow coming while you establish yourself. Also, if your current job offers a benefits package that includes insurance and retirement, that may be an incentive to keep your online travel business as a part-time operation. Starting part-time gives you the opportunity to gain experience and build a solid reputation as a travel specialist. Some individuals continue working part-time indefinitely, while others wait until they have built up enough cash reserves to sustain them during the first year's full-time operation.

Once readers have decided on the specialty area or niche they want to work with, the first task they face is setting up a multifunctional website. You will be shown several ways to approach this concept, including self-design, outsourcing, and turnkey operations. The second—and probably most difficult—task is learning how to market your business and website to its greatest potential. If you are flush with cash, you can outsource the marketing; however, the majority of readers probably have limited budgets and need to learn how to do the legwork themselves. And that is where this book will come in handy.

The most important thing that readers need to be aware of is the continually evolving world of internet marketing and how that can impact their business. What you don't know, your competition will, so you always want to be on top of their game. This book will not only serve as a guide to a fast-growing industry that many people enjoy, it will also provide you with a game plan and resources you can put in action right away.

Throughout the book, you'll hear from our featured online travel entrepreneurs who have started their own businesses. These folks have built successful careers online and have invaluable insights to share with you. And later in the book you can read about their interesting backstories.

What you won't learn is how to get rich quick or become an overnight success. Being an online travel specialist requires hard work, dedication, and commitment. That's what running a business is about. You're going to love parts of the process, and you're going to learn to like other parts. As for the rest—you're simply going to learn.

Chapter 2

Finding a Travel Specialty or Niche

*P*eople enter into an online travel business from many different avenues. Most have a strong interest in traveling—whether family destinations, cruises for singles, walking across Europe, or organizing business events. They may be

➡ creative travel enthusiasts with a special niche they would like to develop.

➡ travel professionals who would like to quickly and efficiently set up an online business.

➡ cyberpreneurs who want to enjoy the freedom of owning a business that is virtually risk-free.

➡ travel agents or tour operators who would like to expand their business beyond their brick and mortar walls.

➡ baby boomers or retirees looking for a second career.

➡ students or stay-at-home parents needing to supplement their income.

Before you can begin any serious business planning, you must first decide what travel specialty you're interested in. As you consider the niche you want to develop, think about your own likes and dislikes, skills and resources. For example, Jenny Reed and her husband decided to take their love for traveling and turn it into a business when they bought a franchise from Cruise Planners (ourcruiseplanner.com). "We started our business seven years ago, and the travel industry has really evolved since then," says Reed. "At the time I wasn't even looking in the direction of an online travel business, but that has proven to be very successful."

You cannot be an expert in every area of the travel industry because it is too vast. But if you narrow your niche to a targeted market, such as disabled travelers, traveling with pets, cruises for women, and so on, you will become known as an expert in that particular field and your business will grow. Making your niche too general can make defining your target audience difficult. On the other hand, making your niche too narrow and specific can reduce your sales opportunities by reducing your target audience.

CLICK TIP

To meet the rapid development in niche travel planning, The Travel Institute (thetravelinstitute.com) has introduced a new line of specialist courses that is an extension of its Destination Specialist programs. Travel professionals have the opportunity to earn a Specialist designation in several niches: Accessible Travel, Adventure Travel, Diving, Gay and Lesbian Travel, Golf, Honeymoons and Destination Weddings, Luxury Travel, Spas, and Yacht Charters.

When thinking about your niche, choose a specialty you are enthusiastic about. It's difficult to maintain motivation when you are promoting a service or products you are not excited about. Of course, if you already have some expertise in a particular field like mountain biking or business traveling, this can be your guide when choosing your niche.

In this chapter you will look at some of the more common specialty areas to see if one might work for you.

Market Research

Once you have chosen your niche or specialty, you will need to do an in-depth examination of your specific travel market. This assessment is essential to your success because it will provide the information that helps you identify and reach your targeted audience, as well as solve or avoid potential marketing problems.

Jennifer Sage (vivatravels.com) researched her intended market by studying every bike tour company she could find on the internet and requesting every brochure possible. "Self-guided tours were just starting to become popular a few years ago, and no one was doing what I planned on doing," she says.

Conducting market research also gives you information about your competitors. You need to find out what they're doing and how that meets—or doesn't meet—the needs of the market. Al DiGuido, CEO of Zeta Interactive (zetainteractive.com), says you need to get a better understanding of how the competitors market their services (i.e., web advertising, search engine optimizing, e-mail campaigns). "They are showing you how they attract their customers," he says. "Learn from them and then work on going to the next level by outperforming their efforts to attract new customers to your service."

One of the most basic elements of effective marketing is differentiating yourself from the competition. One marketing consultant calls it "eliminating the competition," because if you set yourself apart by doing something no one else does, then you essentially have no competition.

However, before you can differentiate yourself, you first need to understand who your competitors are and why customers might patronize them. Offering something no one else is offering could give you an edge in the market—but it could also mean that someone else has tried that and it didn't work. Don't make hasty decisions. Do your homework before finalizing your services. Use Figure 2.1: Travel Niche Worksheet on page 21 to help you define your target market.

DEFINING YOUR SERVICES

Whatever type of online travel service business you decide to start, you'll undoubt-edly discover that your clients come from diverse backgrounds and across socio-eco-nomic lines. Focusing on a particular lifestyle is another way to streamline your travel niche. Some of those sub-niches might be:

- Families
- Singles
- Retirees
- Baby boomers
- Leisure travelers
- Business travelers
- Adventure travelers
- Luxury travelers
- Thrifty travelers
- Gays and lesbians
- Honeymooners
- Students
- Travelers with special needs or interests

Often these are exceedingly busy individuals who need assistance planning the many facets of a complex trip. Or they may be looking for adventure cycling around the French countryside and don't know where to start. Just know that when clients con-tact you, they are not only asking you to find the best options and the best prices, but they are also counting on your guidance. Your insight and the ability to make good recommendations based on your clients' needs and preferences will be your most valuable asset.

DEFINING YOUR SERVICES, CONTINUED

The types of services typically offered by a travel professional may include

- offering one-stop shopping for all travel arrangements.
- creating itineraries and travel schedules that mesh with clients' interests.
- ferreting out the best prices and schedules.
- booking airline tickets and reserving seats.
- booking cruises and cruise/tours.
- reserving hotels and other accommodations.
- arranging for rental vehicles and other ground transportation.
- creating specialty tour packages and possibly serving as the tour leader.
- arranging customized events, like conventions or destination weddings.
- offering travel insurance.
- advising clients about passport/visa requirements, travel advisories, inoculation needs and other domestic and international travel requirements.
- acting as a travelers' advocate (fighting for consumers' rights; assisting travelers with special needs, intervening with suppliers when problems arise).
- coordinating the million or so other details necessary to ensure clients' satisfaction.

CLICK TIP

A majority of people who plan their leisure travel online use the internet to do more than half of their trip planning, according to "E-Travel Consumers: How They Plan and Book Leisure Travel Online." Sixty percent of them rely on the internet for driving directions and maps; 53 percent use it to book hotels, motels, or bed-and-breakfast inns; and 41 percent use it to shop for air fares. Six in ten also say they have used their computers to book travel in the past year, spending an average of more than $2,100.

Travel Specialty Areas

When you have an online business you have the world at your fingertips, which makes niche marketing more important than ever. The travel industry is probably more diverse than most. Because there is an amazing amount of ground to cover, this book is not going to attempt to cover it. However, it is going to focus on a few areas that seem to be of significant interest to many travelers, and hopefully to you.

Adventure Travel and Outdoor Excursions

Adventure means different things to different people. For some it might be sailing or snorkeling in the crystal indigo waters off the coast of Cancun, Mexico; others might get a thrill from petting a shark or climbing 4,000 feet in the cockpit of a Soviet jet trainer. It certainly means a lot of fun for a lot of people. Statistics provided by the Travel Industry Association (TIA) show that during the past five years, 98 million adults have taken an adventure trip—rock climbing, mountain hiking, whitewater rafting, spelunking, parasailing, skydiving, and other activities. "Soft adventure" vacations are milder and may feature walking, bicycling, fishing, camping, or horseback riding.

Many adventure and ecotour operators have developed their niche because of a desire to share their passion and experience with others. Jennifer Sage, owner of Viva Travels, plans custom guided and self-guided bicycle tours in France and Italy. "I love to share my love of traveling by bicycle with others," she says. "I firmly believe there is no better way to see a country!"

Bear in mind that if you're not an expert in a particular outdoor or adventure field, you're not going to have much success. For example, you certainly don't want to attempt navigating the Outback if you've never been there. Sage concurs. "Whether my clients are riders who want easier rides

CLICK TIP

Peter Geisheker, CEO of The Geisheker Group (geisheker.com), recommends research to find out what travel destinations are most popular. He says a great website for researching the world's top tourist destinations is the World Tourism Organization website at unwto.org.

and lots of sightseeing, or whether they want the challenge of climbing the most famous passes of the Tour de France, I can help them because I've done it all."

Luxury Travel

While the explosion of do-it-yourself internet travel booking sites like Expedia and Orbitz were once thought to be a bad omen for the travel agent, a number of recent reports have shown that the field is experiencing new strength. A recent PricewaterhouseCoopers study reported in *Forbes* concluded that large numbers of affluent travelers have given up on using the internet to book their own travel and are turning to travel professionals, because they "want the human interaction"—and are willing to pay for it.

Luxury traveling caters to a posh demographic and does not have any competition from the thousands of discount travel sites. Affluent customers are willing to spend more to get more, which means a luxury travel specialist will need to resonate with people who consider exotic travel to be a lifestyle. Like any other specialty area, you should be familiar enough with your targeted market to make a lasting impression by providing travel experiences that are unique, vibrant, and supremely comfortable. The well-to-do consumer enjoys five-star resorts in trendy destinations, along with experiencing native cuisine and local attractions. They also place considerable importance on personalized service and attention to details.

Many upscale travelers are retaining agents who act as "travel concierges," making all the arrangements from travel and lodging to dinner reservations and theater tickets, often for a flat fee of up to $1,000. Even more well-heeled clients might opt for a members-only travel concierge like a New York City firm that charges $250,000 just to join and another $10,000 in annual fees. Recent articles in such publications as *The*

> ### CLICK TIP
>
>
>
> The Bureau of Labor Statistics reports that the median annual earnings for travel agents in 2006 were $29,210, with the top 10 percent earning more than $46,270. Self-employed agents often have smaller earnings as they are getting established, but stand to earn upwards of six figures at the upper end of the scale, particularly those who cater to high-end luxury travelers.

New York Times and *Philadelphia Inquirer* also note an increased demand for personal service from travel agents as an antidote to the frustrations of do-it-yourself planning and booking on the internet.

Dane Steele Green of Steele Luxury Travel (steeletravel.com) created a very specialized niche within the luxury travel category when he saw there was a need in the marketplace for a luxury, upscale travel company that catered to the gay community. "It's all about luxury," says Dane. "These are people who have the money to experience the finest in life, without having to book it and do all of the work themselves. That's what I do." And he does that by planning

HIGH ROLLERS TAKE TO THE SKIES

One emerging trend travel agents in the luxury segments are reporting—or in some cases retooling to meet—is a rapidly growing interest in chartering jets. No longer the exclusive domain of the super-wealthy, booking a private plane is not only within the reach of many travelers these days but also a strategy that can generate healthy commissions for travel agents, according to an October 2007 article in *Travel Agent*, an industry trade publication. Agents can collect commissions of as much as 25 percent.

An August 2007 *Forbes* article noted the same trend, reporting that the number of private jet operators worldwide had grown from 100 in 2003 to some 500 in 2007. Rising frustrations with commercial airlines may be one major factor in both business and leisure travelers' move toward chartered aircraft, but declining prices also play a part. In 2007, costs to charter a jet that could carry three to five passengers ran about $2,200 an hour; the same plane five years earlier cost $3,800 an hour.

Other considerations for chartering a jet are the safety and quality standards, which are of the highest, as well as availability and flexibility. There are no blackout dates, and one can be available for takeoff with only a couple of hours notice. A charter jet also has the ability to use smaller airports that are less-congested and often located closer to the client's destination.

exclusive, custom-made travel packages and taking his clients to popular destinations around the world—in style.

Cruising Along

Cruises are one of the hottest segments of the travel industry as new and exciting excursions are departing from a wide range of ports. In addition to a fun variety of dining opportunities, spacious suites, and top-rate entertainment, cruises also provide the opportunity to visit exotic locales around the world.

There are many cruise lines designed to accommodate many different lifestyles and special interests such as families, singles, couples, sports fans, gamblers, wine connoisseurs, and music lovers. Sometimes the cruise is developed around a theme such as Carnival's NASCAR voyage or Holland America's social dance events.

The older population is still the mainstay of the cruising industry. Statistics show that almost 70 percent of the passengers on traditional cruises are seniors. To accommodate the more refined tastes of these customers, many cruise ships offer activities such as ballroom dancing, wine tastings, and shore excursions that highlight cultural and historic places of interest. Their port destinations are longer treks to regions like Scandinavia, the South Pacific, or the Mediterranean.

The Business Traveler

Business travel can mean big business for the travel specialist. Executives are busy people, and many are glad to turn over the exhausting details of planning their trips to a competent travel professional. Most large corporations have their own in-house travel departments, so your focus would be on smaller companies. You could offer one-stop shopping, including ticketing and itineraries, or operate as a concierge who coordinates meeting events, makes limo arrangements, and arranges kid-friendly activities while mom is at a conference. Become familiar with the convention and visitor travel bureaus in the major cities that your clients frequent so that you can locate nearby hotels, restaurants, and attractions. The more you know about an area, the more your clients will want to take advantage of your services.

An example of a travel business targeting a specific subset of travelers is MeetingUniverse.com, a niche travel site for business travelers and meeting planners. Its focus is on providing information and ratings to its subscribers about hotels in various cities around the country. This information can be very helpful to meeting planners looking for the right venue for their next conference.

Chris Lopinto, co-founder of ExpertFlyer.com, also caters specifically to the business traveler by providing specialized information usually only accessible to travel agents. "Your niche has to be different, unique, or at least something interesting that is done in a better way than anyone else is doing," he advises. "If you see a hundred other people doing it, don't be the hundred and first to do it."

For Women Only

Recently, *Road and Travel* magazine reported that women influence 85 percent of all travel decisions and comprise 40 percent of all business travelers. "Girlfriends getaways" have become a booming trend in the travel industry, spurring new start-ups like Chick Vacations (chickvacations.com), owned by Heather Hills. When she created the site in 2007, Hills wanted to show women they don't need to spend a lot of money on fancy "raft the Amazon" or "climb the Himalayas" adventure travel. "A weekend girls' getaway doesn't need to be expensive to be a great opportunity to bond with other women," she says.

Another female demographic to target is older women. According to the recent statistics provided by the U.S. Census Bureau, mature women outnumber men by a ratio of 100 to 81 (55–64); 100 to 82 (65–74); 100 to 69 (75–84); and 100 to 49 (85+). The Travel Industry Association of America predicts older female travelers will be one of the driving forces behind senior traveling in the long term.

Although spas and cruises remain popular choices for women, dozens of other special interest trips are springing up: wine-tasting in Napa Valley, making handicrafts with the locals in Costa Rica, or shopping in Versailles.

For both safety and companionship, many women prefer to travel in small groups instead of alone. Beth Whitman (wanderlustandlipstick.com) has written an excellent guide for women traveling solo titled *Wanderlust and*

Lipstick: The Essential Guide for Women Traveling Solo, and this year will release two more books under the Wanderlust and Lipstick series: *For Women Traveling to India* and *For Women Traveling with Children*.

Mancations

"Mancation" is one of the latest buzzwords in the travel industry, a spin-off on the girlfriends getaway marketing phenomenon. Although the term is new, the concept isn't—as evidenced by the dozens of guy-getaway themed movies that have been around for ages. Many of you may remember hearing the reference for the first time when Vince Vaughn's character in the movie *The Break-Up*, said the only vacation he had ever been on was a mancation.

Last year when James Hills was helping his wife, Heather, launch Chick Vacations, he discovered the field of guys getaways was virtually nonexistent online. "A lot of buzz was starting to generate, and we knew this was going to be a good subject," he says. "We took some of the same philosophy from Heather's site and applied it to the Man Tripping site (mantripping.com) to show that guys getaways don't need to be booze-soaked orgies. There is a lot more to being a guy than sex and drinking, so I am looking forward to exploring and promoting that angle."

Mancations provide the opportunity for men to get together and bond with guys from work or old friends from college. Although golf outings, sports events, and fishing trips are the mainstays of male bonding, some of the fellas are branching out with high-velocity adventures like skydiving and bungee jumping, while others opt to kick back with spa treatments and back waxes.

Honeymooners

Couples who are deeply immersed in wedding plans are often more than happy to turn over the reins of planning a honeymoon package to a travel professional. The couple generally knows where they want to go and may sometimes have a vague idea of what to do when they get there, but the rest may be up to you. Once you have a sense of their likes and dislikes you can then make some recommendations—whether its cruising in the Bahamas, kanoodling in Hawaii, or camping in the Rockies. Upon their arrival, surprise them with a spa treatment basket, champagne on ice, or tickets to a special attraction.

Unique personal touches and attention to details will increase the odds you'll be recommended to family and friends.

Senior Travel

Today's seniors have better health, wealth, and education, along with more time on their hands than previous generations. They have become the leading influence in the travel industry and marketers are swiveling around to pay closer attention. Demographic trends are clear. According to statistics provided by the TIA, the mature market (55+) will gain in travel intensity over the next 20 years.

Anticipated long-term trends are increases in adult-only travel parties, declines in travelers looking for traditional family experiences, more soft-adventure tours with outdoor activities, and interest in local heritage and culture. Senior travelers are becoming more independent, preferring less group travel. However, they still want well-organized agendas and pre-arranged transportation. This particular niche represents a tremendous opportunity for travel entrepreneurs who want to target the market.

Grandtravel

"Grandtravel" is a specialized niche that is one of the fastest growing travel trends, representing more than 21 percent of all trips taken with children last year, according to the TIA. Grandparents today are not like grandparents of yesterday; greater numbers are more energetic, active, and adventurous. They don't want to stay home and look after the grandkids. Instead, they want to pack the kids up and take them along on fun-filled vacations, while leaving the parents at home to take a breather. Because geography separates many families, special trips bring grandparents and grandchildren together to strengthen bonds and create lasting memories. As an added bonus, most of the time senior and children's discounts can be factored into the package for added savings.

Disabled Travelers

Travelers with disabilities have more opportunities than ever to explore the world with the assistance of hi-tech support and creative planning. A study done by the Open Doors Organization, the TIA, and the Society for Accessible Travel and Hospital (SATH) indicates that disabled travelers currently spend approximately $3.3 million a year on travel. "Dialysis cruises" using portable dialysis equipment are planned for patients and their families; road trips are taken with wheelchair accessible vans and buses; and transportable nebulizers and oxygen cylinders are made available for travelers with respiratory problems.

When planning a tour for those with physical limitations, consider the accessibility of the facilities on your itinerary. Are there steps that will need to be navigated? Even one step could be a problem for someone in a wheelchair or using a walker. Does the museum have elevators large enough to accommodate wheelchairs? Are the restrooms in the basilica handicapped accessible? Are aisles and walkways at the quaint little antique village wide enough for wheelchairs and scooters? Are the sidewalks in the town rough and uneven?

As each country has its own standards, disabled clients traveling abroad may face additional challenges regarding transportation and accessibility. Advance research and planning are a necessity so your clients can have a safe and enjoyable trip. Provide international travelers with disabilities copies of the pamphlets, *New Horizons for the Air Traveler with a Disability* and *Plane Talk: Facts for Passengers with Disabilities*, that can be ordered from the Department of Transportation (see next paragraph).

Make sure disabled clients know their rights when traveling and know what to do if they encounter discrimination. Contact the Department of

CLICK TIP

The Society for Accessible Transportation and Hospitality (SATH) works to promote awareness, respect, and accessibility for disabled and older travelers. It is part of its mission to educate the travel, tourism, and hospitality industry to be more accessible for people with disabilities, in accordance with the Americans with Disabilities Act of 1990 and the Air Carriers Access Act. For more information, visit its website at sath.org.

Transportation by calling 202-366-4000 or visiting its website at dot.gov for a list of steps taken by the U.S. government to ensure the civil rights of people with disabilities when traveling by air, ground, or water. This information also covers the use of service animals.

Travelers with Pets

Traveling with pets is a very specialized niche that is growing quickly as demand increases and resources expand. According to TIA, more than 29 million Americans traveled with their favorite canines and kitties during the last three years. Pet lovers cross all economic spectrums, but luxury and business travelers are more likely to spend the extra cash and make the necessary arrangements to bring their beloved companions with them.

Loews Hotels was the first national hotel brand to welcome pets with their "Loews Loves Pets" program. Fido and FiFi even have their own room service menu with recipes prepared from scratch. Since then, many vacation resorts and hotels have added "pet-friendly" to their list of amenities because they realize animal lovers who travel with their pets usually have money to spend. Focusing on this particular trend has given them a distinctive edge over the competition that you can take advantage of.

There are many ways to segue into this niche. For example, you can be a pet travel concierge like Puppy Travel (puppytravel.com) or a subscription-based site that provides up-to-date information for its members at Pets on the Go™ (petsonthego.com). When planning trips for pet lovers you will want to map out dog-walking routes, pet-friendly restaurants, pet shops, groomers, and find information about local veterinarians and other services for the discriminating pet owner.

Shopping Expeditions

Everyone loves a great bargain, especially ardent shoppers who can turn a shopping spree into the ultimate challenge. According to the Travel Industry Association, approximately 55 million people plan trips around outlet-mall shopping each year. But why stop at the mall? Preplanned shopping missions can be anywhere from a day trip to San Francisco's Chinatown to a weekend jaunt in the Amish Country to a fortnight browsing for antiques in Brussels.

Historical Jaunts

In a recent survey by the Travel Industry Association and *Smithsonian* magazine, 81 percent of travelers reported including cultural, arts, and heritage activities in their trips. This was confirmed when last year more than 53 million tourists pursued historic and cultural interests. These included museums, galleries, battlefields, cities, and other sites. As a tour operator, you can plan historical vacations to see the Roman ruins in Tunisia or visit Renaissance festivals in the Carolinas. The possibilities are endless as well as educational and fun!

Specific Age Groups

When defining your target market, you may want to narrow your focus to a specific age group, such as: senior adults (born before 1946); baby boomers (1946–1960); generation X (1961–1979); generation Y (starting from 1980). Each group has different dynamics and needs. By becoming a specialist in that market, your business can expand to meet the travel needs of that age group.

Group Packages

Andi McClure-Mysza, president of the Independent Contractor Division for Montrose Travel (montrosetravel.com), feels that group travel is probably one of the most profitable ways travel agents or tour operators can run their business. She recommends targeting specific markets for advertising purposes. "Perhaps you want to promote a group cruise that's all about health and fitness," she says. "Sign up the personal trainer at a local gym to be the featured speaker and guest on the ship. Then ask the gym to give you its mailing list or let you piggyback on a mailing it's already sending out." Not only do you have 50 people

CLICK TIP

For more information on how to learn more about the nuts and bolts of starting a travel and tours business, including finding host agencies and specialty travel carriers, see Entrepreneur's start-up guide *Start Your Own Travel Business and More* written by Rich Mintzer.

PLAN OF ACTION

As with any type of start-up business, an online business requires a plan of action or an e-business plan. This is really your blueprint for success that will guide you over the course of the next seven days and beyond.

So what goes into an e-business plan? Here are some ideas to get you thinking in the right direction:

➡ What is the purpose of your online travel site?

➡ Who are your targeted customers?

➡ Are you providing a service, product, or information?

➡ How competitive is the market? (High, medium, low)

➡ Who is your competition?

➡ What vendors or suppliers will you use?

➡ How will sales be handled—through the vendor, supplier, or you?

➡ Will your website need a shopping cart portal and a means of handling credit card information?

➡ What is your online promotional/marketing strategy?

➡ What is your offline promotional/marketing strategy?

➡ What is your strategy for customer satisfaction?

➡ Who handles website development—will you do everything yourself or out-source some of the elements (i.e., site design, content writing, search engine optimization)?

A business blueprint will also tell you if you need funding, something I'll talk more about in Chapter 12 (Financial and Business Management). Chances are you will not. A product-based business often requires inventory, which requires cash. But if you are a service-oriented business, you will find that it's easier to get by without financing. A homebased online operation that only has one employee (you) does not generally need extra funding unless you decide to quit a well-paying, full-time job to focus exclusively on your online travel business. In that case, pull up Entrepreneur.com's Starting a Business website that has a special section for writing effective business plans (entrepreneur.com/businessplan).

signed up for the health and fitness cruise, but you have 50 potential customers who might be taking their own vacations in the near future.

Figure 2.1: **ONLINE TRAVEL NICHE WORKSHEET**

How well have you defined your targeted market? This list can help you get organized and coordinate your efforts:

Identify three specialty areas you would like to target:

1. _____

2. _____

3. _____

What specific skills do you have in those areas? _____

_____

_____

Will you need additional training or education? _____

_____

_____

What additional equipment will you need? _____

_____

_____

Figure 2.1: **ONLINE TRAVEL NICHE WORKSHEET,** CONTINUED

Identify your clients: _____

_____

_____

What services/products do they need? _____

_____

_____

Who is your competition? _____

_____

_____

How will your services/products be different? _____

_____

_____

Chapter 3

Choosing an Online Travel Business Model

*T*hanks to the internet, e-commerce has put its indelible stamp on the business world by completely revamping how various companies and entrepreneurs operate and producing different business models. Naturally, to avoid confusion it's important to decide which model you are going to use for your online travel business.

In this chapter you'll look at several of the more common online business models that could be beneficial to an online travel business. These models do not need to be used in isolation. Some online business models overlap and complement each other, and many businesses use two or more models concurrently to great effect. However, if you are just starting an online business, beginning with one model makes life much simpler. Once you have your business up and running successfully, then you may want to experiment with complementary business models.

Setting Up an E-Commerce Site

Perhaps the most obvious online business model is the e-commerce or merchant model, which was the first to really take off on the internet. This is used to sell merchandise or services online that are your own products or sold through an affiliate program. With this model you provide a website containing information about the various products or services you are selling as well as an ordering mechanism (i.e., shopping cart) so that customers can select and pay for the products they want.

Using the e-commerce model, you can reach a far wider audience than with a physical store, thereby increasing the opportunity for sales. Your customer base instantly expands from your local town or state to the entire online world. There are, however, many facts to consider to target a global audience—shipping options and costs, the shelf life of products if they will be shipped across the globe, and the international standards products may need to meet.

CLICK TIP

To see a comprehensive and definitive list for starting a new business, take a look at StartupNation's "Ten Steps to Open for Business" at startupnation.com/pages/start/10Steps.asp.

dards products may need to meet.

Do some research to find out whether other people are selling similar products online and whether there is a high enough demand for your product or services. Check out the practicalities in terms of inventory, order processing, and shipping before you make the decision to pursue this type of business model.

Information or Content-Rich Site

The information or contact-rich site is probably one of the easier types of online business models to launch. Anyone can set up an information site, typically a blog. You just need to spend a little time finding a niche that is both interesting for you and profitable in terms of information products or advertising.

Information or content-rich websites and blogs provide the customer or user with up-to-date and detailed information about a particular subject. There are two ways that you can use this type of online business model to generate revenue: (1) by directly selling the information to customers, or (2) by providing the information for free and using advertising related to the niche subject to create income. Some online businesses successfully combine these two strategies.

Web Advertising Model

To use this model you need a website that has a dozen or more pages of well-written and informative content applicable to your travel niche. You can then add relevant advertising to your site in the form of banners, sidebars, and text links, which may generate an income either when they are viewed, when they are clicked, or when they are clicked and your visitor completes a specified action such as making a purchase or signing up for a newsletter.

For this strategy to provide a significant income, you either need to generate a large volume of traffic to the site or have highly specialized advertising that pays well for each viewing or click. Using an AdWords campaign is one of the simplest ways of generating revenue through web advertising, and this service enables you to

> ## Words of Wisdom
>
> *Setting a goal is not the main thing. It is deciding how you will go about achieving it and staying with that plan.*
>
> —Tom Landry,
> coach of the Dallas Cowboys

do detailed research into the potential payouts for ads in your niche subject area. There's more about how to effectively use Google AdWords in Chapter 7.

Where Does the Content Come From?

Depending on the topic, your budget, and the type of revenue generation you are aiming for, there are a number of ways to generate content for your articles and website. The following are some suggestions:

➡ Write the content yourself. If you are a specialist in your niche subject, enjoy researching topics, and have good writing skills, then writing your own content is the best option. That way you can be assured of the quality and accuracy of the information presented, plus it doesn't cost you anything.

➡ Find someone to write the content for you. This is a popular alternative for people who would rather spend time marketing their site than writing the content or who aren't confident in their writing skills. Copywriters and researchers can be found online using service brokers such as Elance (elance.com), Guru (guru.com), or other specialized freelance copywriting companies that produce original content.

➡ Use existing content. There are a number of online businesses selling or giving away public label rights (PLR) content, such as article directories. Some of these articles are sold to a limited number of customers so they are published by relatively few websites. This is good to avoid duplicate content penalties with the search engines. Many sites publish articles that you are allowed to download and use on your site for free as long as you provide a link back to the author's site. This is a good way to generate quality content—especially in the beginning—but should not be the only source of information on your site. Not only do you need original content, but you want to avoid having a lot of material that may be reproduced on other sites because this would ultimately lower your rankings in search engine placements.

➡ Use an infomediary. An infomediary, or information intermediary, provides information about a particular market, set of products, or group of consumers. Analysis, reports, and information from these sources can be particularly useful if you are selling information products rather than using the advertising model. Usually you have to pay for the information because these providers have invested a lot of time and research. But if you can reuse it in an original and engaging

INFORMATION IS A HOT COMMODITY

Selling information products on a content-rich website can be an excellent way to generate income online. The information can be in the form of e-books, reports, articles, how-to guides, or videos. Draw in visitors by offering free content like a destination travel e-guide or product reviews. Not only does this content whet their appetite for more, but it also demonstrates that you are an expert in your field.

You need to ensure that your information and content is up to date, and produce new information products to keep visitors coming back for more. You will also need to market your site to keep traffic levels high. Of course, having a sincere personal interest in your niche when setting up your website or blog will make this concept much easier.

For ideas on how to generate content for your website, read the Article Marketing section in the Essentials of E-Marketing chapter.

format, you can charge a good price for your information product, which will make the investment worthwhile.

Membership or Subscription Site

The membership or subscription business model is gaining popularity online because of the perceived value that comes from receiving information and services that only members have access to. Revenue is generated through a membership site when members pay a recurring subscription,

CLICK TIP

It can take some time to start making a significant profit from an information site. However, once you have a site that is producing a good income, you can repeat the same formula on several other sites, resulting in a fairly high profit relative to your investment.

either weekly, monthly, or annually, to gain access to restricted areas of the site and the exclusive information or services contained within those areas.

Some membership or subscription sites have "teaser" sections that are free to visitors in the hopes it will persuade them to become subscribers. For example, a freebie area may provide a handful of relevant articles as well as a comprehensive list of other articles for which only summaries can be viewed by nonmembers. Some membership sites have various levels of membership, with bronze members having limited access to basic information, forums, and so on, and silver or gold members paying higher fees and having more perks and unlimited access.

MyTripJournal.com is a membership-based travel site that offers a free advertising-supported version or a premium-paid, ad-free version to its members (see Figure 3.1). Dan Parlow, CEO and co-founder, says currently it is earning more revenues from the subscription fees, although he feels the ad-supported version will be more profitable in the long run because more people will see them. "We have two types of visitors to our site," says Parlow. "Some people are coming to view their friends' and families trip journals. Then there are other people who are searching through journals on a destination basis or vicariously traveling through other people's shoes."

The level of subscription fees for membership sites depends greatly on the other revenue streams the site has. If subscription fees are the only revenue stream and all the information and services are free thereafter, then the subscription fees are likely to be quite high. If the site includes advertising or sells information products in addition to subscription fees, the fees should be lower so as to attract more members and increase the other revenue streams. Some sites even charge a one-time membership fee with lifetime access thereafter because they focus more on other revenue streams than on subscriptions.

WARNING

Before investing a lot of time and money into an online business venture, be sure you have the expertise, budget, and resources required at your disposal. Scale back on your plans, if necessary, until you are in a better position to expand.

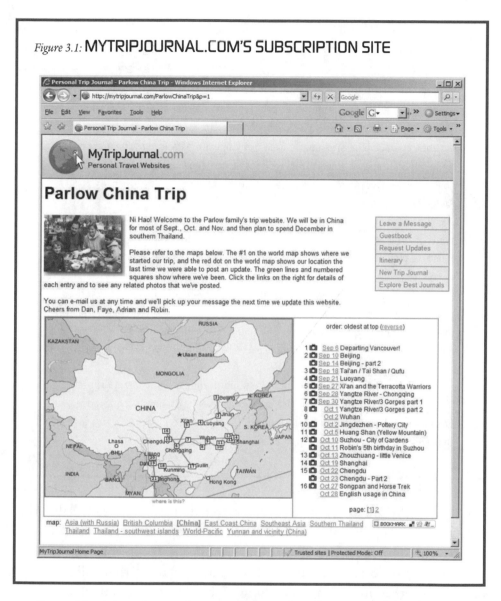

Figure 3.1: MYTRIPJOURNAL.COM'S SUBSCRIPTION SITE

ExpertFlyer.com is another good example of a successful subscription-based model. Co-founder Chris Lopinto attributes the site's success to the fact it is doing something distinctively different that targets a specific niche: business travelers and frequent flyers. "It's advantageous to do subscriptions because it's guaranteed income," he says. "But you have to make sure what

IT'S ALL IN THE COMMUNITY

An online community is a group of people who share common interests and contribute views and information via a specific website. Users of these community sites usually need to register as a participant in order to contribute, which makes tracking their usage of the site much easier. Many operate as a forum where experts and laypeople can discuss specialized topics and exchange advice. Their popularity is obvious given the astronomical rise of social networking sites such as MySpace, Facebook, and LinkedIn.

Starting up a community website is similar to a membership or subscription site. Members provide most of the information and content for the site, so maintenance is low. But you will need to provide some fresh material and monitor the site to ensure it is properly utilized and managed. People who contribute to the forums on a regular basis develop a strong sense of loyalty, which you want to encourage so they will return frequently. This is why online communities are great for well-targeted advertising, which is how most community sites make their revenue.

A community site alone does not produce a profit, unless you charge a subscription fee to belong. However, you can use additional revenue streams such as advertising or selling products relevant to your community because you have a captive audience that will return again and again, making it a quite profitable model.

you're doing is unique, and that your targeted customers really value that information." Lopinto also adds that the subscription fee needs to be low enough that people are not going to really notice it. "People will spend $5 or $10 on a cup of coffee or lunch, so this is not something that will hurt their budget. Plus they are getting something of value for that nominal fee."

Working with a Host Agency

As a travel specialist, you can sell airline tickets if that is part of your business plan; however, you may not actually write them unless you are already a brick-and-mortar travel agency looking to expand your business online. To write tickets you need to have an appointment from the Airlines Reporting Corporation (ARC), and they do not grant appointments (which are like licenses) to an agency that is not housed in a commercial office space. So how do you sell airline tickets? Rich Mintzer offers a detailed explanation in *Start Your Own Travel Business and More* (Entrepreneur, 2007):

Most homebased travel agents affiliate themselves with a host agency, which is a commercially-based outfit with an ARC appointment. The travel specialist is an independent contractor—sort of a freelance salesperson—finding and maintaining his or her own clients, selling travel products to them, and then splitting commissions with the host agency. When clients need airline tickets, the agent makes the arrangements but has the host agency do the actual ticket printing.

This is a terrific relationship that works well for everyone involved. The travel professional doesn't need to worry about that elusive ARC appointment, and the host agency gets additional profit with a minimum of extra work.

The real reason this relationship is a winner is there are so many more products that can be sold than airline tickets, and these products pay much higher commissions. Tours and cruises of all sorts abound, and the companies that provide them pay commissions of 10 percent or more. Since many of these products are priced much higher than airline tickets, selling them is a lot more lucrative than selling seats on planes.

Montrose Travel (montrosetravel.com) is a family-owned and operated travel agency that also operates as a host (mtravel.com) for homebased travel agents, with more than 320 travel professionals

> ## Words of Wisdom
>
> *Be creative. Use unconventional thinking. And have the guts to carry it out.*
>
> —Lee Iacocca

under its umbrella. "An individual could technically join us today and call themselves a travel agent tomorrow," says Andi McClure-Mysza, president of the Independent Contractor Division for Montrose Travel. "Of course they have to pass the criminal background check first. And we want to make sure they are serious about running a travel business and not just looking for personal discounts."

Like most host agencies, Montrose provides its agents with many different services, including ongoing training, accounting and technology support,

---

HOW TO CHOOSE A HOST AGENCY

Rich Mintzer (*Start Your Own Travel Business and More*) offers these tips on how to choose a good host agency.

One of the best things you can do is talk to other agents who work with a host agency and find out if it is paying its commissions on time and giving the support that the agents need.

The goal is to find a host agency that is not a card mill, but will provide you with the travel suppliers and support you need. Mainstream hosts belong to organizations like The Outside Sales Support Network (OSSN) and National Association of Commissioned Travel Agents (NACTA); card mill people don't because they are not welcome. To find a list of legitimate host agencies, visit the Professional Association of Travel Hosts Inc. (PATH) at pathonline.travel.

You also want to find out:

- ➡ how long a host agency has been in business,
- ➡ if it is properly licensed and bonded,
- ➡ what kind of support and/or training it offers,
- ➡ what its commission breakdown is (and if there are any deductions),
- ➡ what associations is it affiliated with (ARC, CLIA, etc.),
- ➡ how many travel suppliers and preferred suppliers it works with,
- ➡ what fees it charges and how often it charges, and
- ➡ how will it communicate with you.

Also make sure it has emergency support and is up-to-date on the latest in technology. PATH also suggests that you check to see if it has $1 million in E&O insurance.

---

errors and omissions insurance, access to the Global Distribution System (GDS), and the ability to issue tickets through ARC. Members are also provided with a professionally designed website that has online booking capabilities, a huge perk for customers who want to handle their own travel arrangements.

"We want our agents to succeed, so we're going to provide them with all of the tools they need," says McClure-Mysza. "We don't make money unless our agents are making money, so our interests are completely aligned."

McClure-Mysza recommends that anyone interested in getting into this part of the travel industry to sign up with a host until they are bringing in $1 or $2 million annually. "There's a whole sub-industry now with host agencies that allows people to establish themselves in a creditable, reputable way."

Of course, you don't have to work with an accredited host agency to provide your clients with airline tickets. You can find the tickets online yourself and have your client pay for them with a credit card. However, a host agency can provide you with the benefit of its established supplier relationships, preferred commissions, and special marketing incentives that would not ordinarily be available to you as an individual.

Expand Your Business on eBay

Selling on eBay is really very simple as long as you approach it systematically. The first step is, of course, to set up a seller's account. Next, choose a selling format. The most popular is eBay's standard online auction format, but you can also sell through your own eBay store (see below) or set a fixed price for your item. Then select your category; write a great title and description; decide how long you want your listing to run, when it should start and end, what your minimum bid will be, and other pricing details; add pictures; enter your payment and shipping information; and then very carefully review your listing. If everything is accurate, submit your listing and you're in business—literally. This is, of course, a very simplistic overview of selling on eBay. If this is a business model you are interested in pursuing, we highly recommend buying Entrepreneur's *How to Start an eBay Business*.

So why should you add eBay as a sales venue to your online travel business? Consider that in 2007 eBay's annual gross merchandise sales exceeded

$60 billion and in the first quarter of 2008, $2.6 billion was sold in the business and industrial category. Statistics like this clearly indicate that eBay provides extraordinary opportunities to reach a worldwide market with different products and services.

Among the many benefits of operating a business on eBay are:

➡ *Targeted traffic.* Through eBay's superb search engine optimization, customers who are specifically looking for your product will be directed to a landing page featuring your eBay store or auction page. With an average of 70 million unique visitors coming to the site each month, this can be a much-added boost to your online marketing campaign. Listing your product or service on eBay will save money traditionally spent on advertising as well as eliminate the difficulty of building and trading links or finding joint venture partners to promote your product.

➡ *Increased sales.* eBay can be used in conjunction with your existing business as an additional selling platform by directing visitors to your non-eBay site. You can sell seasonal vacation packages or promote a new travel product to a huge audience by listing it on eBay.

➡ *User friendly.* Setting up as an eBay seller is probably one of the easiest things you can do as part of your business. You are guided through every

CLICK TIP

Before taking the plunge and starting a full-fledged website, many companies test the waters by selling products and services on eBay first.

step of the process. Creating a seller's account is free although you have to provide specific information that can be verified as part of eBay's fraud-prevention measures. There are also helpful communities and discussion forums on eBay and the internet that answer questions and help you enhance your online selling skills.

➡ *Test marketing.* eBay is an effective site to use for testing the market to determine demand and price points for various products.

➡ *Tools of the trade.* eBay wants its sellers to be successful so it provides a large variety of tools to make businesses as profitable and efficient as possible. There are also many third-party tools available as a direct result of eBay's impressive growth.

eBay Stores

Along with putting merchandise or services up for auction on eBay, you may want to consider opening an eBay store, which would allow you to sell your fixed price and auction items from a unique destination on eBay. Currently there are more than 300 travel service businesses operating as eBay stores, and more than 20,000 stores sell travel-related products.

In addition to making it easy to cross-sell your inventory and build repeat business, eBay stores offer a convenient selling platform for all your eBay listings—auctions, fixed price items, and store inventory. eBay promotes stores in

LEVEL WITH ME

eBay offers three store levels: basic, featured, and anchor. All have their own customizable storefront and the ability to list store inventory, but featured and anchor stores have additional services. Check the eBay website for current store subscription fees. Here's how the three levels differ from one another:

➤ *Basic*. Your store is automatically listed in the eBay stores directory and appears in every category directory where you have items listed.
➤ *Featured*. Your store rotates through a special featured section on the eBay stores homepage, receives priority placement in "related stores" on search and listings pages, and is featured within the category directory pages where you have items listed. In addition, you receive monthly reports on your sales and marketplace performance.
➤ *Anchor*. In addition to the services offered to featured stores, your store can be showcased with your logo within the eBay stores directory pages and will receive premium placement in "related stores" on search and listings pages, which means your store will be placed higher on the page than the featured stores.

several ways. All your auction listings will contain the eBay store icon; when bidders click on that icon, they are taken to your store. That icon is also attached to your eBay user ID for increased visibility. The eBay store directory is designed to promote all stores and drive buyers to your particular store. You also receive your own personalized eBay store website address that you can distribute and publicize as you wish.

The cost of a basic eBay store is a nominal monthly fee (current rates can be found at ebay.com) that increases with the level of services you desire, along with additional fees for items listed and sold.

The Pros and Cons of Franchising

If you like the idea of starting a business straight "out of the box," then a travel services franchise could be your ticket to success. With this tried and true concept comes brand name recognition that has a proven working model, an enthusiastic team of go-getters, and comprehensive hands-on training. In other words, although you are in business for yourself, you're not alone.

How It Works

In a nutshell, the franchisor lends a trademark or trade name and a business model to the franchisee, who pays a royalty and often an initial fee for the right to do business under the franchisor's name and system. The contract binding the two parties is the franchise, but that term is also used to describe the business the franchisee operates.

The best part is the franchisor has already worked the kinks out of the system and is available to help franchisees when new challenges arise. According to the Small Business Administration, most businesses fail from lack of management skills. This is less likely to happen with a franchised

CLICK TIP

If you're considering a franchise, visit the International Franchise Association website at franchise.org. You can search for details on more than 1,200 franchises, learn franchising basics, and participate in discussion boards with other franchise seekers and owners.

business because your franchisor is there to guide you through the maze of business ownership.

Typically you think of fast food and restaurants when you think of franchising, but virtually every business form has the potential to be franchised, and there are a number of franchised travel businesses. Jenny Reed bought her franchise from Cruise Planners seven years ago and has enjoyed tremendous success over the years. Reed feels that belonging to her particular franchise is very beneficial because of the steady stream of support and information the franchise owners receive. The franchise program also has an excellent marketing department that provides a web program like the one you see on her site (ourcruiseplanner.com). "Although I have the ability to customize certain web pages and add new pages, I don't have time to keep the content and everything up-to-date," she says. "Fortunately Cruise Planners will take care of that for me." And although cruise lines have optional marketing programs, owners have the ability and freedom to be creative, think outside the box, and do other types of marketing because they are independently owned and operated.

The Cons

While there are many benefits to owning a franchise (security, training, and marketing power), there are some drawbacks. Perhaps the most significant is the cost of a franchise. The initial franchise fee for an online travel business can run anywhere from a few hundred to several thousand dollars. Then you have continuing royalty payments to the franchisor, payments based on the gross income of your business. Additional expenses may include promotional and advertising fees, operating licenses and permits, insurance, and other costs of running a business.

Another big drawback is that you have to give up some of your independence. Each franchise is different on how firm their conditions and requirements are; however, you will be bound by the contract to follow and implement the rules and procedures established by the franchisor. For example, if you neglect to pay your royalty fees or misbehave by not meeting performance standards, your franchise could be terminated and you may lose your investment. So, if you like to make your own decisions and "do your own thing," a franchise may not be right for you.

CLICK TIP

Much of the information you'll need about a franchise will be provided in the form of a document known as the UFOC, or Uniform Franchise Offering Circular (ufocs.com). Under Federal Trade Commission (FTC) rules, you must receive and review this document before you are asked to sign any contract or pay any money to the franchisor.

You also have no control over how the franchisor operates, and the corporate office can make decisions that you may not agree with or that may even reduce your profitability. That's why it's so important to thoroughly research a franchise; you want to see a positive operational pattern before making a commitment.

Buying an Existing Business

An alternative to a franchise or to starting your own business is to take over an existing online travel business. Generally this type of business can be purchased lock, stock, and barrel with a developed website with an established domain and integrated with search engine optimization—and most importantly—with a client base.

While this may seem like a simple and logical shortcut for anyone starting a new online travel business, note that there are drawbacks to buying an existing business. Though the actual dollar amounts required depend on the size and type of business, it often takes more cash to buy an existing business than to start one yourself. Plus when you buy a company's assets you may get stuck with some of the liabilities as well. Find out why the business is for sale. Don't accept what the current owner says at face value; do some research to make an independent confirmation.

Why do people sell businesses, especially profitable ones? There are a variety of reasons. Many entrepreneurs are happiest during the startup and early growth stages of a company; once the business is running smoothly, they get bored and begin looking for something new. Other business owners may grow tired of the responsibility or have health or other personal issues that moti-vate them to sell their companies.

You'll find a variety of businesses for sale advertised in trade publications, in local newspapers, on the internet, and through business brokers. You can also find existing businesses for sale on Craigslist (craigslist.com) and eBay (ebay.com). Although it's highly unlikely that you'll find an existing business that is precisely the company you would have built on your own, you just might find the business you want is currently owned by someone else.

Drop-Shipping

It's possible for you to carry items on your website that you don't already own and will never actually take possession of. Here's how it works: You find a dis-tributor of products you want to sell, such as luggage or travel accessories, and promote these products on your website. (Note that you don't have to sell everything the distributor does.) When an order comes in, you process the payment (retail price plus shipping) and then send the order to the distribu-tor, who ships the product directly to your customer in a package that shows you as the shipper on the label. The distributor bills you the wholesale price plus shipping and handling. You make a profit, the distributor makes a profit, and the customer is happy and comes back to buy more. It really is that simple.

This process is known as "drop-shipping," and it is a long-standing busi-ness practice. It's a win-win. You don't have to stock inventory, handle the product, pack, ship, and so on, and the distributor doesn't have to worry about retail sales.

Of course, you have to choose the right merchandise for your online travel site and deal with reputable distributors. If anything goes wrong your cus-tomer will hold you responsible, even though the drop-shipper may be at fault.

Avoid drop-shippers who want to charge an account setup fee or insist on a minimum monthly purchase. Be sure that they are factory-authorized wholesalers of the brands they represent, and that the goods they are shipping are brand-new, factory-warranted products.

WARNING

Do your research on your suppliers so you can avoid getting involved in a broker "daisy chain" (a chain of brokers who are each marking up the products). There is nothing wrong with buying from brokers or distributors, but you should always know who the actual seller is and be able to contact the seller directly, if necessary.

While it may sound as easy as 1-2-3 to shoot an order over to the manufacturer—who will package and ship the product while you collect the proceeds—this process has its flaws. For example, a customer may receive goods that were damaged during shipping and look to you for restitution. You then file a claim with the manufacturer, who blames the carrier for careless shipping, who blames the manufacturer for inadequate packing, and nobody is happy—especially the customer. If this appears to be a recurring theme, you may decide it's more advantageous to be a hands-on kind of seller and take care of packing and shipping yourself or find a new distributor.

Know Your Specialty

Identifying your specialty and then determining the online business model that would be most suited to that field is crucial to your success. Although the amount of work and investment varies from one business model to the next, all of them require a high level of commitment and regular maintenance to be profitable. Because of the anticipated involvement with your online travel business, make sure it revolves around a niche you enjoy and a business model you can enthusiastically embrace.

Chapter 4

Building Your Website

*T*oday, an internet presence is as essential as a telephone and fax machine. A website is your online brochure, and it will be working for you 24 hours a day, seven days a week. In addition to credibility, a professional looking website gives you a variety of marketing opportunities that will be discussed in great detail throughout this book. Whether you decide to set up and design your own website or hire someone to do it for you, there are some things you need to think about in advance.

A Name to Remember

One of your best marketing tools is the name of your online travel business. A well-chosen name can work very hard for you; an ineffective name means you have to work much harder at marketing your business.

The first and most important thing is deciding on a name for your online business and registering a primary domain name. Your business name should very clearly identify what you do in a way that will appeal to your target market. If it's too obscure or cryptic, people will have no idea what your business is. Make the name short, catchy, and memorable. It should also be easy to pronounce and spell. People who can't say, write, or type your business name may use your services, but they won't be able to tell anyone else about you.

Though naming your company is without a doubt a creative process, it helps to take a systematic approach. Use Figure 4.1: Business and Domain Name Worksheet on page 49 to help you work through this process. Once you've decided on a name, or perhaps two or three possibilities, check to see if any other business has the same or similar name by doing a search on Google.com.

Jennifer Sage says she came up with the name for her travel site because of the way it resonated. "I've always loved the sound of the word 'Viva!' she says. "It conjures up exciting, memorable, lively, and fun moments."

Using Your Own Name

Many entrepreneurs use their own name for their business, which has several benefits. One is you don't have to trademark your name because it's already

---

CLICK TIP

Visit Nameboy (nameboy.com) to find clever and interesting domain names in your area of specialty. This is a great free nickname generator that can be used for finding names for almost anything, although it is primarily used to find domain names for websites. Simply type in two keywords that best describe your business and let Nameboy do the rest.

yours. And chances of it being registered as a domain are a lot slimmer. Using your own name not only improves your personal credit as your travel business grows, but it will build prestige within the community. It won't take long for people to recognize your name and associate it with your business.

Just for fun let's see what we can do with the name Sandy Beaches. Not only is "Sandy Beach" a well-known park on the South Shore of Oahu in Hawaii, but you might be surprised to know how many people actually have this name. As part of this exercise, let's say that Sandy is a travel writer and blogger. A short list of possible combinations might include:

1. Sandy Beaches Writing
2. Sandy Beaches Travel Blog
3. Sandy Beaches, Travel Writer
4. Beaches Travel Writing
5. Traveling with Sandy
6. Writing by Sandy Beaches
7. Sandy Beaches and Friends
8. Sandy Beaches Travels
9. Globe Trotting with Sandy

This list could easily grow by a couple of dozen names, but this gives you an idea of how to get started by changing elements around. With one exception, these names all clearly indicate what type of venture this is. However, number 7 is too vague, making it unclear what services are provided. And number 8 is going to be buried ten pages deep in search results because "sandy beaches" and "travels" are commonly used keywords in the travel industry. (More on using keywords in the SEO chapter.)

So what if your name is something that doesn't roll off the tongue very easily, like Euthanasia Pididiot? Or it has an unpleasant connotation like Robin Banks or John Crapper? (Yes, these are names of real peo-

CLICK TIP

For an in-depth look at different strategies you can use to improve your website, download *10 Ways to Improve Your Website* a free, comprehensive, 54-page report from Entrepreneur.com. Go to: entrepreneur.com/downloads/10ways toimproveyourwebsite.pdf.

ple.) Or worse, what if someone else has the same exact name for their business? Relax. This is the part where we crank up those creative juices and have some fun. Actually, the name "Creative Juices" has been used for several businesses. But not to digress, use Figure 4.1: Business and Domain Name Worksheet on page 49 and follow along as we guide you down the path of inspiration.

Selecting Your Domain Name

Think about your target market and do a search on similar niches within your business area to see what keywords consistently pop up. Next, look at potential domain names by visiting a registration site like register.com. This site is particularly helpful because not only can it tell you if the name you've chosen is available, it offers a list of alternatives if it is taken.

Ideally your domain name should be the same as your online travel business. But in the event that domain is taken or is too long, the URL of your website should still clearly and accurately reflect the nature of your travel business. It should also be 22 characters or less so it's easy for people to remember. The fewer characters the name has, the less likely it is that people will make a mistake when typing the address into their browser.

If you find that your preferred domain name has been registered by someone else, you have the option of placing a backorder on it in the event it becomes available in the future or making an offer to the current owner. But before investing big bucks in what may seem like the perfect name, try playing around with alternatives. For example, although you cannot add spaces you can insert a hyphen or underscore in between words like this:

mydomainname.com
my-domain-name.com
my_domain_name.com

It's important to note that domain names cannot include punctuation marks such as periods, colons, or exclamation points. Also, forward or backslashes are not allowed. Domain names are not case sensitive so capitalizing one or two letters won't help; however, you can change a letter or substitute a number. A couple of examples are:

CLICK TIP

While some SEO experts believe that it's advantageous to register a domain with keywords and hyphens in the URL, many now believe it to be a disadvantage because of spammers. It's not surprising to see crazy URLs like cruises1-cruises2-cruises3-cruises4.com. However, all of the experts agree it's a good idea to include keywords in the URL *after* the domain like this: traveling4business.com/meeting-venues.htm.

marystraveldealz.com
traveling4business.com

Drop Catchers

Another alternative to finding the ideal domain name is by catching one that has been dropped by another e-tailer. This happens when someone allows their domain to expire—whether consciously or by mistake. Industry experts say that approximately 200,000 expired domain names become available every day. The domains are quickly snatched up by hundreds of companies like Sedo.com (sedo.com) or SnapNames.com (snapnames.com) to be sold or auctioned off. To cast a wider net for "expired domain names," simply type that phrase in your browser's search box.

Of course you want to make sure that you don't become a victim of "The Drop" by following these helpful steps:

➡ *Keep your contact information up-to-date.* Renewal notices are sent to the contact information listed on the account. This includes your physical mailing and e-mail addresses. Notices usually start going out 90 days in advance, with frequent reminders following until the domain is either renewed or expires. The good news is that most registrars give their customers a 30-day grace period after the expiration date.

➡ *Use automatic renewal.* Most registrars offer an automatic renewal service by keeping a current credit card on file. Just remember to update the card in the event it expires or needs to be replaced.

> ## WARNING
>
> Be sure the domain name you are considering is not unintention-ally offensive to someone else. For example, does it have another meaning in a different language? Are letters being used for an acronym that has an unpleasant connotation? Just make sure the general public does not associate it with anything unpleasant.

➡ *Register for more than one year.* Probably the simplest way to protect your investment is by registering your domain for more than a year at a time. Currently, website owners can register their domains for up to 10 years with a considerable cost savings.

➡ *Use an active email account.* You are strongly discouraged from using a free e-mail account when registering a domain name. These accounts are often closed if they haven't been accessed in 30 to 90 days. Also, adjust your spam filters so that your registrar's e-mails always make it to your inbox.

➡ *Put the date on your calendar.* Mark the date of your domain's expiration on your calendar to help remind you when it's coming due.

Domain Extensions

The news flying around the internet lately would have us believe all the domain names are being gobbled up and pretty soon there won't be any left.

> ## CLICK TIP
>
> Still having trouble coming up with a name that is just right? Seek out the help of professionals such as NameStormers (namestormers.com). For a flat, fixed fee they will help you find a "name to remember" to give your product or service the attention it deserves.

That would be an erroneous belief. Sure, the most desirable names with the popular .com extension are being registered as fast as they are thought of, but there are still millions of accessible domain names. And as more domain extensions are introduced, the possibilities are expanding.

Also, keep in mind that you are not limited to registering just one domain name. It's actually a good idea to register your domain name with multiple extensions to protect

COMMON DOMAIN EXTENSIONS

For inquiring minds who would like to know exactly what a domain name extension or TLD (top level domain) is, it's the final part of a domain name following the period. The granddaddy of all domain name extensions has been and will probably always be ".com." The dotcom carries a lot of clout because it's typically what surfers will type into their browser if they don't know or can't remember another extension.

Although .net is not used as often, it is considered to be the second most valuable extension for domain name syntax. Other common extensions are .org, .info, and .biz. In addition, there are also country codes used as extensions such as .us (United States), .uk (United Kingdom), .jp (Japan), .de (Germany), and .ca (Canada).

.com—represents the word "commercial"

.net—represents the word "network"

.org—represents the word "organization"

.biz—represents the word "business"

.info—represents the word "information"

.edu—represents the word "education"

.mobi—short for "mobile" and is used for sites designed to be viewed on mobile devices

.us—represents the "United States"

.tv—commonly used for sites within the entertainment or media industry

.name—specifically for personal use by individuals using their own name

your brand. Decide which extensions are the most suitable to your business and snag the available ones, especially .com and .net if they are not taken.

You may also want to register multiple domain names if it's one that generates common misspellings, or if you are selling more than one product or service through your website. Each name can be something different designed to target a specific audience. Then you can have all of the registered domains "forwarded" to your main website.

Registering Your Domain Name

The next step in this process is to register your domain name as quickly as possible before someone else beats you to the punch. This can be done through many different venues, including GoDaddy.com, Register.com, and NetFirms.com. Different registrars charge different prices and offer different packages, so look closely at several to see which one best suit your needs.

New domain registrations typically cost $9 to $35 per year, which generally includes free parking (in the absence of a website), several e-mail accounts, mailing lists, and other e-commerce options. Some of the packages may also include website hosting for free or a nominal fee.

The person registering the domain, the technical contact, and administrator can all be the same person; just remember to provide up-to-date contact information. You should also take this opportunity to make the registration information private by "locking" it—usually for an additional fee. Not only will this prevent spammers from looking up your personal information in the WHOIS database, but it will thwart others from stealing and transferring it.

CLICK TIP

If someone else registers your domain name such as your ISP or another agency, make sure they don't inadvertently register the domain in their name and not yours. This common practice can cause a lot of problems down the road, especially if they let it lapse or sell it to someone else.

Registering Your Business Name

Some states require that you register your business name before opening a business bank account or applying for a loan. This Fictitious Name Statement or Affidavit creates an accurate record of who is responsible for that business. The exception would be if the name of your business was also your legal name. Registering is a simple process that requires a small processing fee and can often be done online. Contact your local county clerk's office for more information.

Figure 4.1: BUSINESS AND DOMAIN NAME WORKSHEET

Try some of these brainstorming ideas to help you come up with a business and/or domain name.

List three (or more) variations using your own name for your business:

1. _____

2. _____

3. _____

List three business name ideas associated with your travel business specialty, product, or niche (i.e., cruises, biking, journaling):

1. _____

2. _____

3. _____

List three business name ideas associated with the geographical area you are focusing on. You can use the name of the town, state, or country. Or use something that area is well known for, such as a destination, wine making, or hiking.

1. _____

2. _____

3. _____

Once you've narrowed it down to a couple of choices, take the following steps:

___ Write it down to see how it looks.

Figure 4.1: **BUSINESS AND DOMAIN NAME WORKSHEET,** CONTINUED

__ Say it aloud to hear how it sounds.

__ Check the first initials of each word to make sure the acronym isn't something inappropriate.

__ Run it by family and friends to see if they are as enthusiastic as you are.

__ Search the internet to see if someone else is using it.

Domain Name Evaluation

Using the ideas above, write down your preferred choices for domain names:

1. _____

2. _____

3. _____

Next, remove the spaces and count how many characters are in each name (excluding the www and dot-extension). If you decide to add hyphens or underscores, be sure to count each one as a character. Ideally you want to keep the name around 20 to 22 characters. You can also include acronyms, if appropriate:

1. _____

2. _____

3. _____

Visit your registrar of choice (i.e., Register.com, GoDaddy.com) to check the availability of your preferred names and determine what extensions can be used. Finally, seal the deal by registering your domain as soon as possible!

Planning Your Site

Before getting bogged down with elaborate web design details, business writer Melissa Campanelli advises entrepreneurs to first sit down and construct a well-thought out website plan. "An outline helps you get the most out of your e-commerce budget," she writes. "You'll know whether you or someone in your company can each do a piece or if you need outside help." Plus, if you decide to outsource some (or all) of the project, a detailed outline will be very beneficial to a professional web designer.

In her book *Open an Online Business in 10 Days* (Entrepreneur Press, 2007), Campanelli provides the following tips for preparing an effective website outline:

CLICK TIP

Make sure the images used on your website are of professional quality. You can use stock photos (istock.com) or hire a professional photographer to create your photos. Image files should be kept as small as possible for quick loading, but not at the risk of losing clarity.

➡ *Content.* The key to a successful site is content. Give site visitors a lot of interesting information, incentives to visit and buy, and ways to contact you. Once your site is up and running, continually update and add fresh content to keep people coming back for more.

➡ *Structure.* Next, structure your site. Decide how many pages to have and how they'll be linked to each other. Choose graphics and icons that enhance the content. Pictures of cruise ships and exotic destinations, for example, might work well if you're promoting cruise packages through a site like Our Cruise Planner (ourcruiseplanner.com). Visitors can click to jump to other pages within the site where they can find more information or book a cruise online.

At this point, organize the content into a script. Your script is the numbered pages that outline the site's content and how pages flow from one to the next. Page 1 is your homepage, the very first page that site visitors will see when they type in your website address, or URL. Arrange all the icons depicting major content areas in the order you want them. Pages 2 through whatever correspond to each icon on your homepage.

Writing a script ensures your website is chock-full of great content that is well organized. Write well, give site visitors something worthwhile for their time spent with you, and include a lot of valuable information and regular opportunities to get more content. Whether you offer a free newsletter, a calendar of events, columns from experts, or travel reviews, content and its structure becomes the backbone of your website.

➡ *Design.* With the content and structure in place, site design comes next. Whether you're using an outside designer or doing it yourself, concentrate on simplicity, readability, and consistency. Before you start using HTML tags right and left, remember what you want to accomplish. Keep surfing the internet to research what combinations of fonts, colors, and graphics appeal to you, and incorporate pleasant and effective design elements into your site. Those little subtleties make all the difference in how visitors respond to your website.

➡ *Navigation.* Make it easy and enjoyable for visitors to browse the site. Use no more than two or three links to major areas, never leave visitors at a dead end, and don't make them back up three or four links to get from one content area to another. For example, if you have a website for convention planners, make it easy for visitors to link to city sites where they can find information about theaters, river cruises, museums, and the like so convention attendees can check out recreational activities on their own.

➡ *Credibility.* This is an issue that shouldn't be lost in the bells and whistles of establishing a website. Your site should reach out to every visitor, telling her why she should buy your product or your service. It should look very professional and give potential customers the same

---

CLICK TIP

Get inspiration for website design ideas by checking out *PC Magazine's* Top 100 Web Sites (go.pcmag.com/topwebsites). You can also find the Criteria for Website Excellence at 100BestWebSites.org, which identifies 21 criteria it uses when selecting top sites.

feeling of confidence that a phone call or face-to-face visit with you would. Remind visitors that you don't exist only in cyberspace. Your company's full contact information—contact name, company name, street address, city, state, zip code, telephone, fax, and e-mail address—should appear on your homepage.

Design Essentials

In today's internet climate, putting together a professional looking site is a relatively easy task, especially with the numerous tools and services available. However, knowing how to structure it and pull everything cohesively together may not be as straightforward as you might hope. Figure 4.2: Web Design Worksheet (found on page 57) will help you sort through and understand the essential elements needed to design an effective website. This worksheet can be used by you personally or by a professional designer if you decide to out-source the project.

The first rule of thumb is to keep things simple "for curb appeal" and ease of navigation. If you start loading up your site with flashy videos and audio features, many of your visitors are going to feel overwhelmed, especially if they are on dial-up and it takes forever for your homepage to download. Plus other computers are not always equipped with the appropriate plug-ins, so separate downloads may be needed to view some of your sites.

If you really feel strongly about using Flash-animated graphics and banners on your site, create two different versions that visitors can opt to use from an introduction splash page. The basic version would be developed for people who have a slower, dial-up connection without all of the bells and whistles. The Flash-enabled site would be designed for folks who have high-speed internet access and can view the special features without any problems.

Another consideration is having your site compatible with the major web browsers: Microsoft Internet Explorer, AOL, Netscape

CLICK TIP

Your time and energy are your best investments and should be used before you invest money into a new business. And don't spend money until you have done the research and have constructed a well-thought-out site plan.

SIX KEY QUESTIONS FOR DEFINING YOUR WEBSITE

Karen Hawkins, owner of Off The Wall Emporium (offthewallemporium.com) for website design, maintenance, and hosting, recommends asking yourself the following questions when defining your website:

1. What are the goals of this website? What do you want it to do?

2. Who is the target audience? Know the demographics such as age, gender, location, socioeconomic information.

3. How will your site benefit your audience? What are you offering people who visit?

4. What is the tone or image for the site? What are the key messages? Are there any themes you want to convey? For example, are there existing pieces the site needs to coordinate with (i.e. printed materials, packaging, signage, logos, etc.)?

5. How do you want the audience to respond to the website? What do you want them to think? Is there something you want them to do?

6. Will the site be promoted? How?

Communicator, and Mozilla's FireFox. Web pages look different from one browser to the next, so it's important to test each page before uploading them to the internet.

The Ten Most Deadly Mistakes in Site Design

In *Start Your Own e-Business* (Entrepreneur Press, 2005), Robert McGarvey and Melissa Campanelli point out there are 100 deadly goofs site builders can make, but they narrowed the focus down to the most disastrous ten. "Avoid these gaffes, and your site will be far better than much of the competition," they write.

1. *Disabling the "back" button.* Evil site authors long ago figured out how to break a browser's back button so that when a user pushes it, one of

several undesired things happens: There's an immediate redirect to an unwanted location, the browser stays put because the "back" button has been deactivated, or a new window pops up and overtakes the screen. Porno site authors are masters of this—their code is often so malicious that frequently the only way to break the cycle is to restart the computer. This trick has gained currency with other kinds of site builders. Our advice: Never do it. All that's accomplished is that viewers get annoyed.

CLICK TIP

Avoid underlining text in your site's content. Typically, underlined text indicates a hyperlink, so other underlining is confusing to site visitors.

2. *Opening new windows.* Once upon a time, using multiple new frames to display content as a user clicked through a site was cool, a new thing in web design. Now it only annoys viewers because it ties up system resources, slows computer response, and generally complicates a surfer's experience. Sure, it's easy to use this tool; but don't.

3. *Failing to put a phone number and address in a plainly seen location.* If you're selling, you need to offer viewers multiple ways to contact you. The smartest route is to put up a "Contact Us" button that leads to complete information: mailing address, and phone and fax numbers. Even if nobody ever calls, the very presence of this information comforts some viewers.

4. *Broken links.* Bad links, that is, hyperlinks that do nothing when clicked, are the bane of any surfer. Test your site, and do it weekly, to ensure that all links work as promised.

5. *Slow server times.* Slow times are inexcusable with professional sites. It's an invitation to the visitor to click away. What's slow? There is no easy rule, but I'd say that any click should lead to something immediately happening. Maybe a new page or image takes a few seconds to come into view, but the process should at least start immediately.

6. *Outdated information.* Again, there's no excuse, but it's stunning how many site builders leave up pages that long ago ceased to be accurate. When information changes, update the appropriate pages immediately, and this means every bit of information, even tiny facts. As a

small business, you cannot afford the loss of credibility that can come from having even one factual goof.

7. *Scrolling text and marquees.* Although these are very cool site-design tools, they can get easily messed up when viewed in different browsers. It's an odd fact, but Netscape and Microsoft Internet Explorer do not display web pages identically. This can be maddening to the viewer who wants to know, now, what you're offering, but finds that the information keeps scrolling off the page. Use these tools in personal pages because they are fun and add liveliness to otherwise static pages, but put them aside when building business pages.

8. *Too many font styles and colors.* Pages ought to present a unified, consistent look, but novice site builders, entranced by having hundreds of fonts at their fingertips and dozens of colors, frequently turn their pages into a garish mishmash. Use two or three fonts and colors per page, maximum. The idea is to reassure viewers of your solidity and stability, not to convince them you are wildly artistic.

> ## CLICK TIP
>
> For some excellent resources on fonts and typestyles,
> visit the Adobe website (adobe.com), The Font Site (fontsite.com), and 1001 Fonts (1001fonts.com).

9. *Orphan pages.* Every page in your site needs a readily seen link back to the home page Why? Sometimes users will forward a URL to friends, who may visit and want more information. But if the page they get is a dead end, forget it. Always put a link to "Home" on every page, which quickly solves this problem.

10. *Using leading-edge technology.* Isn't this what the web is all about? Nope, not when you're guaranteed to lose most of your viewers whenever your site requires a download of new software to be properly viewed. Never use bells and whistles that force viewers to go to a third-party site to download a viewing program. Your pages need to be readable with a standard, plain-Jane browser, preferably last year's or earlier. State-of-the-art is cool for techno wizards but death for entrepreneurs.

Figure 4.2: **WEB DESIGN WORKSHEET**

Domain Name/URL: _____

Web Host Name: _____

    Account Name: _____

    Password: _____

Online Travel Business Description (approximately 200 characters)
This brief, descriptive information will be used when submitting your site to search engines.

_____

_____

_____

_____

Keywords
Think of common keywords and phrases used to describe your site/business. They can be specific or general. These words will be included in content and page headings for search engine crawlers to pick up.

_____

_____

_____

Figure 4.2: **WEB DESIGN WORKSHEET,** CONTINUED

Target Market (i.e. age range, interests)

_____

_____

_____

Purpose of Website

❑ Provide information about services/products

❑ Directly sell products/services

❑ Strengthen brand identification

❑ Develop a list of clients/prospects

❑ Other (please explain): _____

Web Pages Needed

❑ Home Page

❑ About Us/Bio

❑ Products/Services

❑ FAQs

❑ Calendar of Events

❑ Links

❑ Contact Us

❑ Guestbook

❑ News/Media/Press

Figure 4.2: **WEB DESIGN WORKSHEET,** CONTINUED

❏ Location/Map/Directions

❏ Privacy Policy

❏ Response/Order Forms: _____

Site Colors

Background: _____

Text: _____

Active Links: _____

Viewed Links: _____

Font Style

Common fonts that are generally supported by all browsers are:

❏ Arial

❏ Times New Roman

❏ Georgia

❏ Verdana

❏ Courier

❏ Identify here if you wish to use other types of fonts: _____

Logo

Indicate if you have a logo or wish to have one created:

❏ Have existing logo

❏ Would like to have a logo created (Note: see GotLogos.com)

❏ Do not want to use a logo

Figure 4.2: **WEB DESIGN WORKSHEET,** CONTINUED

Existing Sites

List below the URLs of sites that are particularly appealing to you. Also identify what you found interesting such as color, style, font, layout, organization, content, etc.

_____

_____

_____

Special Features Needed

❏ Discussion/Chat Forum

❏ Blog

❏ Newsletter

❏ Shopping Cart

❏ Flash

❏ Video

❏ Audio

Hosting Your Site

Now that you have this great website put together and ready to launch, let's talk about your hosting options. Unless you plan on hosting it yourself (not a typical option due to cost and operational factors), you will need to find a reliable web host provider.

A web host stores your website, including graphics, and transmits it to the internet for other users to view. Not all web hosts are created alike, so shop around for one that has the best package for your needs. Some will include freebies such as domain registration, design templates, or no setup fees. And most hosts provide combination packages that can include site-building tools, content management, shopping carts, product catalogs, tracking and reporting capabilities, e-mail accounts, and more.

Depending on how much disk space you need, basic hosting service can start as low as $8 per month. How do you determine the amount of disk space your site requires? It really depends on the size and number of images you

PAID HOST VS. FREE HOST

Free is good, right? Not when it comes to website hosting. A "free" host is never actually free. The host has to make money somehow, and the most common way is with those annoying, flashy banners and pop-up sponsor ads that have absolutely nothing to do with your business but are going to be the first thing visitors to your site see. You have absolutely no control over the ad content, and some of it can be quite inappropriate. You'll also find that most free hosts offer very little, if anything, in the way of technical support.

Free sites are typically very limited in the amount of space you have. Most allow no more than three pages and minimal use of graphics, resulting in very plain, unprofessional-looking sites without the extras that a paid host provides. Finally, your URL will be long and clearly indicative of the fact that you are operating from a free site, such as myfreewebhost.mygreattravelsite.com. Unfortunately, this does little to inspire confidence in your customers. A good web host doesn't have to be expensive. There are a lot of good, affordable hosting services out there, and many provide packages that include a registered domain name, professionally designed templates, secure services, e-mail boxes, online or phone support, and more.

have on your site. Most sites do not use more than 10MB of storage, and most web hosts offer between 10MB and 35MB of free storage with the option to upgrade. But if you are still in doubt, check with a computer consultant before committing yourself to a specific plan.

Special Features

Aside from looking professional, the best thing about your website should be its content. This is the substance that will entice visitors to linger and browse around your site, and come back later for more. Keeping in mind that simple is better, below are some advanced tips and tools to help you present the content a little more advantageously.

CGI Scripts

CGI stands for Common Gateway Interface and is a programming tool that allows small applications to run on websites. They can be used to track visitors, install guestbooks, launch discussion forums, implement forms, and a host of other interesting features. Although you can create a CGI script from scratch, one would have to wonder why when there are thousands of free ones for the taking. An excellent resource is The CGI Resource Index (cgi.resourceindex.com).

Polls/Surveys

Surfers have never hesitated offering their opinions when asked, so ask. When used effectively, polls can be an excellent way to build reader loyalty and drive

---

WARNING

Spammers try to infiltrate guestbooks by harvesting e-mail addresses or leaving messages with links back to their sites. The best way to get around this annoyance is to use a guestbook that requires registration or a system where the poster needs to enter text generated from an image. Also, set up your guestbooks so that users' e-mail addresses are not published.

---

traffic to your site. One example is to place a poll widget on your home page once a week and ask visitors generic questions like "Have you ever gone skinny-dipping while on vacation," or "Do you use a camera phone when traveling." Lonely Planet (lonelyplanet.com/travelpoll) has a great selection of fun travel polls that include the final results. Free poll templates and widgets are available through SurveyMonkey.com (surveymonkey.com) and FreePolls.com (freepolls.com).

Guestbooks

Although guestbooks are considered a bit outdated, many people prefer to utilize this simple technique of allowing visitors to leave their names and comments. Plus it's an easy and convenient way to collect more information about potential clients. Whenever someone takes the time to sign your guestbook, it is usually an indication they were interested in your products or services. Encourage guests to write a review or ask questions in their comments. This information can provide you with new ideas on how to improve your site. Reply to their posts with a personal thank you (not an automated response) and include a small plug endorsing a product or service. Look for some free and fee-based guestbook templates at Bravenet.com (bravenet.com) and Smart Guestbook (smartgb.com).

Message Boards and Chat Rooms

Get to know your visitors better by adding an interactive message board or chat room to your website. A message board (a/k/a discussion forum) helps to establish a sense of community among frequent visitors, while providing information to newcomers who can often look back in the archives for previously discussed topics. Message boards also have the advantage of being monitored to prevent spam messages or inappropriate discussions taking place. Chat rooms can be spontaneous and fun, but if your site is not generating a lot of traffic in the beginning, there will not be a lot of chatting going on. Another disadvantage to having a chat room is that it needs to be carefully monitored during the times it is open. An alternative to a chat room is to sign up with an AOL Instant Messenger account (aol.com) so that visitors can ask you questions whenever you are online.

Site Search Tool

If your site is rich in data with a lot of pages, visitors would definitely appreciate the use of a search box to find relevant information. Adding search engine capabilities to your site can be as simple as installing a prewritten code to downloading comprehensive software. Google now has a customizable search engine that can be placed on your website or blog that is operational within minutes. It can even be used in conjunction with the AdSense program. For more information about site search tools, visit Search Tools (searchtools.com). This helpful site has a wealth of information and advice about products, news, and technology.

Privacy Policy

Junk e-mail and the risk of being a victim of online fraud may make some people reluctant to sign up for a newsletter or purchase products from your travel site. To allay these fears, have a clearly-written and prominently placed privacy policy that states how you will both use and safeguard personal information. If cookies are being used to track visitors, you need to disclose this information. Likewise, if you plan on sharing or selling your customer's contact information to third parties, you will need to divulge that little tidbit too.

The most effective privacy policies are short, to-the-point, in plain English (not legalese), easy to find, and easy to understand. For free assistance in composing your own policy for your site, visit Web Dev Tips (webdevtips.com/webdevtips/codegen/privacy.shtml) and the Direct Marketing Association (the-dma.org/privacy/creating.shtml).

FTP (File Transfer Protocol)

This is an easy method used for transferring web pages to a web server. If your web host does not provide an FTP service, you can download a low-cost, easy-to-use version through Ipswitch (ipswitch.com) or CuteFTP (cuteftp.com).

Shopping Cart

This is a program with specially designed software that handles the e-commerce section of your site by letting customers purchase and pay for products or services online. If your web host does not offer a shopping cart solution, use the free, multifunction e-commerce solution offered through PayPal (paypal.com).

Chapter 5

Turnkey Websites and E-Commerce Solutions

*U*sing a turnkey solution is probably one of the easiest and quickest ways to launch your online travel business. And sometimes it can be very cost-effective. When considering whether or not to buy a turnkey website, think about your professional goals. This can be a great option if you want to establish a strong web presence but don't have the time or the skills required to design your own site.

Turnkey websites have been created for the cyberpreneur who has limited knowledge of web programming and is anxious to start his business. Whether you use a company to customize your website or utilize one of the many turnkey applications available, you can be up and running in less than a day.

What Is a Turnkey Website?

Turnkey sites come from the idea of the "turnkey project," a term that has been used for decades. The origin of the term comes from the implication that all the customer has to do is "turn a key" to be in business, with all the necessary equipment and supplies needed to run the store in place.

> ### Words of Wisdom
>
> *Not having a website is akin to being in business and not having company stationery, a telephone, lawyer, accountant . . .*
>
> —FROM *MADSCAM: KICK-ASS ADVERTISING WITHOUT THE MADISON AVENUE PRICE TAG* BY GEORGE PARKER

A turnkey website has been fully developed for a specific product or service. This means the site has been designed, supplied, built, and installed to completion. It is fully loaded and ready to go at one convenient price. Generally the purchase includes original website design, web hosting services, installed scripts for forms, shopping carts, affiliate programs, and even search engines optimization so as to achieve a higher search ranking.

Outsourced E-Commerce Solutions

Many providers can offer a total e-commerce turnkey solution that includes design and creation of the website, hosting, online marketing, customer support, payment processing, and order fulfillment. These professional web designers and marketers have vast experience and skills in creating sites that are not only visually appealing but also technically superior with excellent marketability. You should note, however, that professionally designed turnkey e-commerce sites can be expensive, particularly the ones that merit attention and are flawless in design. Businesses that typically utilize this type of solution generally have a high-sales volume because outsource costs are steep. Fees can range anywhere from $1,000 to $10,000, depending on the

CAUTION: NOT ALL TURNKEY PROVIDERS ARE CREATED EQUAL

There is always "one bad apple in the bunch," and on the World Wide Web there are usually more than a few. So use caution when selecting a provider. Some turnkey website services charge exorbitant prices for basically "cookie cutter clone" websites that are standardized and impersonal, so do your homework before making a big investment. Remember your goal as an up and coming webmaster is to create an original site that has new and relevant content on the subject of your business. Consider the following tips before choosing a turnkey website service to improve your web presence:

➡ *Look for a turnkey internet business that offers a return on your investment.* Some of these companies will go so far as to offer a guarantee of ROI or your money back. Additionally, professional companies will happily offer full training so that you can effectively manage your site, along with ongoing technical support.

➡ *One of the reasons to avoid standardized websites is because sometimes these sites are actually subdomains of a parent website.* This may not be noticed by casual internet browsers, but it will be noticed by some search engines, which will lower your ranking.

➡ *Additionally, some companies will standardize your web copy, which means search engines will find duplicate content in your website and in other websites the company has developed.* This will have a negative impact on your search rankings, regardless of specialized SEO work done, since original content is very important to ensure a high ranking. Therefore, make sure that the site offers original content and high quality writing.

➡ *Carefully review the company's parent website and go by your first impression.* After all, this is the site that is selling its own web designing services. Does it seem sharp or sleazy? Be wary of any company using sensational marketing techniques and hyperbole. Simple case in point: lots of adjectives, giant fonts, exclamation points, talk of overnight millionaires, and an almost

CAUTION: NOT ALL TURNKEY PROVIDERS
ARE CREATED EQUAL, CONTINUED

desperate tone that offers secrets to outstanding web success should all be seen as black flags.

➡ *Look at the company's contact information*. This is often a telling sign about the legitimacy of a company. Be suspicious if a company only provides an e-mail address or post office box and refuses to provide real names, physical addresses, or even phone numbers.

number of special features added. And some providers also require a revenue share of 20 percent or higher.

E-Commerce Turnkey Solutions

Many e-commerce entrepreneurs who want a more hands-on experience turn to web hosting companies to help with their e-commerce needs. Typically, companies such as Yahoo! Merchant Solutions, GoDaddy, and eBay offer a combination of services including tools for site building, content management, and product catalogs, along with shopping cart technology, multiple payment options, marketing strategies, tracking and reporting capabilities, domain registration, and web hosting.

eBay

Whether you are buying or selling, you will find that eBay (ebay.com) is an incredibly user-friendly system. Chances are you have already browsed around and may have completed some transactions. Even if you're unfamiliar with eBay, the site itself will take you through the process quickly and efficiently.

From a buying standpoint, eBay offers a vast number of products for the travel professional. For example, if you enter the word "travel" in the search box, the results will show hundreds of auctions promoting luggage, clothing, vacation packages, and more. This is important to know because of eBay's phenomenal affiliate program offered through Commission Junction (cj.com), which is discussed in Chapter 10, The Travel Affiliate.

Of particular interest are the turnkey websites available for immediate purchase and download. These sites come fully stocked and loaded with programming, graphics, and shopping carts. Some have been optimized for the search engines and have their own domain name. Others have booking capabilities and affiliate programs that may also be integrated with Google AdSense.

Communicate with the eBay seller to find out what type of ongoing support is offered upon completion of the sale. Often these are sites offered by professional web designers who will continue to provide hosting and other essentials. However, sometimes these sites are resale (cloned) packages with little or no support—or value.

WARNING

Before signing up with any turnkey e-commerce solution, visit some of the online sites that are using the services of a specific provider, such as Amazon WebStores, to see how you like the final product. Browse around to see how easy it is to navigate and test drive some of the available features on those particular sites. Often, these providers will offer a 30-day trial period.

ProStores

Another way to create an online presence is by using ProStores (pros-tores.com), a complete e-commerce solution for retailers that is a subsidiary of eBay. ProStores, not to be confused with eBay Stores, are independent websites that come fully loaded with e-commerce and merchant capabilities and easily integrate into the eBay marketplace. These stores have their own shopping carts, product catalogs, merchant capabilities, and many other features that can be customized to suit your needs.

ProStores are also compatible with eBay, allowing you to easily create auction-formatted or fixed-priced listings on eBay whenever you want from your website, or vice versa by copying eBay listings directly to your ProStore.

Although sellers are responsible for marketing their stores, more customers will be driven to these stores, thanks to eBay's search engine optimization. If you have a lot of products and want to have an off-eBay store in addition to a presence on eBay, this is a convenient way to do it and have everything tied together.

Depending on your online travel business needs and budget, ProStores offers four levels of service ranging from $9.95 to $249.95 per month, along with transaction fees on each sale:

1. *ProStores Starter.* This is a good low-cost solution for newcomers or individuals with limited products to sell. PayPal is the only accepted method of payment and tech support is available through e-mail only.

2. *ProStores Business.* This is a good, customizable solution for small businesses that includes search engine optimization, personalized domain, tech support 24/7 via e-mail or phone, and multiple payment/checkout options.

3. *ProStores Advanced.* This setup has been designed for medium-sized businesses that have a lot of products and/or services (up to 50,000) and need advanced promotional, merchandising, management, and payment processing features.

4. *ProStores Enterprise.* Designed for "enterprise" type businesses that want to add an online presence to their brick-and-mortar operation. In addition to all of the other features, this level also includes vendor and

CLICK TIP

When looking for a web hosting company, consider choosing one that will solve all of your e-commerce needs. Ideally, it should offer features such as a full wizard-driven setup, many templates, a database-driven system, and payment beyond PayPal.

sales team management, drop shipping, affiliate programs, and multiple buyer groups.

Yahoo! Merchant Solutions

Yahoo! Merchant Solutions (smallbusiness.yahoo.com/ecommerce) offers a wide variety of e-commerce solutions, including clever wizards that streamline the design process and put together a professional-looking site within minutes. A small set-up fee is required to start the process, followed by a monthly charge and transaction fees based on the type of plan you select.

In addition to the wizards and templates, you will also receive 24/7 customer support, a shopping cart, options for processing payments and orders, web hosting, e-mail addresses, and enhanced security. Perhaps one of the best features of Merchant Solutions is that each developed web page follows a standard coding format, making it easy for the search engines to find and index your site. Each page also has a static URL that can be customized with relevant keywords to improve its rankings. The plans currently available are:

1. *Express*. This plan has all of the basic features mentioned above and is great for the entrepreneur who has just a handful of products or services to sell.
2. *Starter*. For the small-to-medium size business with a large volume of products to sell. Additional features include inventory management tools, store set-up, a merchant account to process credit cards, and the ability to promote your own affiliate programs.
3. *Standard*. For the medium-to-high volume business that needs additional product promotions such as cross-selling and gift certificates, real-time integration when processing orders, and the ability to batch process shipments through UPS.
4. *Professional*. For the high-volume business that generates sales in excess of $80,000.

Amazon WebStores

Amazon has a 1-Click WebStore program (webstore.amazon.com) that allows users to quickly and easily build a website within minutes. It includes scripts, flash designs, and numerous widgets—all for one moderate monthly fee (plus transaction fees). Additional features are search engine optimization, credit card processing, e-mail campaigns, and fraud protection through Amazon's world-class fraud protection program. WebStores also offer the ability to upsell Amazon products through an Associates Program and receive referral fees. Another perk is that you can create multiple stores and still pay the same monthly rate. This is beneficial if you are promoting several packages, brands, or services. Visit the site to see a website demo or sign up for a free 30-day trial.

Do-It-Yourself Software Applications

Thanks to advanced, innovative, and reasonably priced e-commerce applications and software that is easy-to-use, many cyberpreneurs feel comfortable building and setting up their own websites. Microsoft has a couple of products that are good choices for designing your own web pages: Expressions (microsoft.com/expression) and FrontPage (microsoft.com/frontpage). Dreamweaver (adobe.com) is another popular software that many users prefer. But if you need a more complete e-commerce solution, including shopping cart functionality, you may want to consider GoDaddy or osCommerce.

CLICK TIP

There are many online website building tools for you to consider using to beef up your site. Business writer Melissa Campanelli reminds us that, "This may be an all-you-can-eat buffet, but the more you put on your plate, the more discomfort your website viewers will feel." So use these tools sparingly.

GoDaddy

GoDaddy (godaddy.com) is the ultimate e-commerce solution for the do-it-yourselfer. The Quick Shopping Cart featuring three different plans makes it easy to create and launch an internet web store (with a shopping cart) that accepts credit cards, offers multiple shipping options, provides hosting and inventory management, and traffic stat monitoring. The best part—no transaction fees! You just pay a monthly rate based on the selected plan and keep all of the profits.

Many other e-commerce options are offered through GoDaddy a la carte such as domain names, web hosting plans, site builders, SSL certificates, e-mail accounts and marketing campaigns, and other business solutions.

osCommerce

osCommerce (oscommerce.com) is an excellent solution for an aspiring entrepreneur who has some web programming knowledge and web design capabilities. Not for the computer illiterate, this site offers an extensive range of innovative features that helps users to set up online stores and websites reasonably fast and easily. Everything is available for free as an Open Source based solution under the GNU General Public License. Basically what that means is there are no copyrights associated with the software. It is free for public consumption. OsCommerce's philosophy is to "provide an opportunity for people to work on software with others that share the same interest, exchanging ideas, knowledge, and work with one another, to expand and improve the solution."

In Summary

Understand that when you purchase a turnkey website, this is not a means to an end. In other words, you still have to work it. A turnkey website is just another tool in your business arsenal, not a springboard to your dotcom "dreams." If you lack a complete business plan and are generally following your heart hoping to learn the logistics of the business along the way, then putting all your faith in a turnkey website company can be an expensive mistake. Used wisely, a turnkey website can be very profitable, but only to a business owner who already has a fully realized vision, with all the necessary equipment, supplies, and professional contacts ready to go.

Chapter 6

SEO: Building Your Internet Presence

*E*ver wonder why certain sites keep popping up at the top of a search query whenever keywords are used? Is there a secret to earning higher search engine rankings? Not really; at least not in the same sense as national security secrets or breaking the magician's code style of secrets. The real secret is learning how search engine rankings work, which is primarily providing relevant keywords, coherent new content, and steadily increasing your incoming links. Fortunately, this information is widely available. We're going to try to condense some of it in this chapter by providing helpful tips about Search Engine Optimization (SEO) as well as free and fee-based marketing strategies.

According to a recent report from the Pew Internet & American Life Project, which provides reports measuring the impact of the internet, 71 percent of American adults use the internet. Of that percentage, at least 91 percent use search engines to find information online. Even without those statistics, everyone knows that people conduct online searches by entering specific keywords into a search engine's search box. But what most people don't know is how some of these sites consistently turn up on the first and second pages of the search results. The page is important because statistics indicate that people will not venture past the second or third page of search results. You have to think like your targeted visitor, so ultimately the goal is for your site to appear in the top 20 search results (ideally top 10).

When James and Heather Hills started planning their sites (mantripping .com and chickvacations.com), they implemented SEO strategies by using tools like KeyWord Discovery (keyworddiscovery.com) and SEOBook.com's Keyword Tool (tools.seobook.com/keyword-tools/seobook), as well just good old-fashioned "googling" for various topics. "We wanted to research and see how well optimized various travel sites were to see if we could compete," says James. They also used Google's Adwords External Keyword tool (adwords

---

CLICK TIP

NYC-based Travel Ad Network (TAN) (traveladnetwork.com) is the leading and largest vertical ad network in travel. This has been a year of extraordinary growth and achievement for TAN. It surpassed Yahoo Travel generating the largest travel information audience online. Delivering 12.5 million monthly unique visitors, TAN has become a powerhouse for advertisers wishing to target travel decision makers and is ranked third by comScore in the overall travel category (which includes transaction sites) and first in travel content.

.google.com/select/KeywordToolExternal; formerly Sandbox Tool) to gauge the relative interest from advertisers on different topics.

To get the maximum benefit of a website, you want it to rank as high as possible in the results when a user conducts an online search. One way to increase your site's visibility is to make it "bot-friendly." The term refers to the "robots" or "spiders" that search engines send crawling through the internet, scavenging information from websites that is indexed for searches. The more information those electronic researchers can access from your site, the higher your ranking will be.

Whenever search engines like Google or Yahoo! produce results from keyword queries, surfers see two different types of links: contextual (paid) advertisement links and natural (free) links. The next section is going to talk about both types in detail, but since browsers typically click the natural links first, that is our starting point.

CLICK TIP

When linking to another site—whether it's within your own site or someone else's—use keywords to describe the link. For example, don't just say "Click here for more information" or give the domain information only. Instead, provide a stronger call to action with appropriate keywords like "You can find more information on our page for *Bed and Breakfast Inns*." Search engines also like when you bold the text of your specific keywords to make them stand out.

Understanding Keywords

The use of targeted keywords is essential in promoting your site through search engine optimization. So, think about what keywords or phrases you would type in a search engine to find a website selling your services or products. The first few keywords will be rather obvious. If the purpose of your website is to sell travel guides, then words and phrases like "travel guides" and "guide books" will be your first words to target. However, there are thousands of sites promoting travel guides, so you will need to streamline your search to include destinations or special interests.

Next, consider other unique, related words your audience might decide to look for, such as "New York hiking trails," "mountain biking books," or "long distance hiking." These are just a sample of the many unique keywords Sue Freeman uses on her Footprint Press Outdoor Recreation Guidebooks site (footprintpress.com).

Plan to use different keywords on various pages of your website. For example, like Freeman, devote an entire page to dog walking trails in and around New York City and another to waterfalls in Canada and the Northeastern United States. Use these keywords with other pages to create a complete website that focuses on all aspects of a particular topic.

Make a list of 25 keywords and phrases that apply to your site, including plural and past tense versions, as well as synonyms. From the list, select a primary and secondary keyword or phrase for one of your web pages. The primary keyword should appear in the title tag, main heading, content of the text, and the linking URL. The secondary keyword should appear in one or two subheadings and throughout the text.

When it comes to content, search engines seem to rank pages higher with relevant keywords in the opening paragraph. A good rule of thumb is to write your content like newspaper journalists who generally summarize the angle of the story at the beginning.

The best way to score a high ranking on the search engines is to provide good, relevant content on your website using unique keywords. Keep the word count around 500 or less and don't stuff the page with keywords. Otherwise,

---

CLICK TIP

When brainstorming for unique keywords and phrases, use a thesaurus like the one at Thesaurus.com to find other words related to your topic. Other helpful tools are Wordtracker's free keyword suggestion tool (freekeywords.wordtracker.com), and Google's AdWord Keyword Tool (adwords.google.com/select/KeywordToolExternal).

the search engines will toss your page into the abyss without cataloging it—they hate spam. They also hate it when webmasters resort to other forms of trickery like using hidden keywords or links (done by making the text teeny-tiny and the same color as the background so only the spiders can see it), or insert irrelevant links or keywords. They will also ban you from future searches if you copy another website's content.

Link Building Strategies

Search engines track how many other websites point back to your site. The more sites featuring your site's URL, the higher your site will rank in search results, right? Well, not exactly. You've probably heard the old adage, "You are judged by the company you keep," and this definitely applies to what sites you link to. Whether you are trading links with another site or including their hyperlinks in your site's content, you want to make sure theirs is a high-quality website that is relevant to your own. If you link to mismatched or inappropriate sites just for the sake of getting backlinks, you will actually do your site a disservice.

Incoming Links (aka Backlinks)

Traffic building through *quality* incoming links is critical for an online business. The more quality sites you have pointing to your site, the better. Note the emphasis on "quality." If the link is coming from a spammy type of site that is trying to acquire hundreds of links in the hopes it will raise its visibility, that doesn't help you at all. However, if the backlink is from a highly reputable site in your niche, that has more clout and gives you higher visibility.

Acquiring quality inbound links is an extremely important part of the SEO process. The sites promoting your links have to be relevant; otherwise, unsuitable backlinks can do more harm than good. Let's say you have a site that caters to female

CLICK TIP

There are a number of online backlink checkers you can use to see who is linking to your site or your competitors, like the one found at iWebTools (iwebtool.com/backlink_checker).

weekend travelers like Chick Vacations (chickvacations.com), owned by Heather Hills. If you have incoming links from an online poker site or one sponsoring medication for erectile dysfunction, the search engines would

HOW TO ACQUIRE MORE INCOMING LINKS

➡ *Search engines*. Submit your site to all of the major search engines. Make sure to read their submission guidelines before proceeding so that your site doesn't get bumped out of line.

➡ *Provide good content*. Give people a reason to link to you by making sure your site's content is useful. Informative and well-written content will always be linked to by other sites. Strategically use keywords and phrases so no one will guess that the text has been optimized for the search engines. Also, the more content the better—but not all on the same page. The more web pages you have indexed with different keywords, the better your chances of showing up in an online query.

➡ *Alert the media*. Send out a press release featuring your site and URL. Submit to online press release services like PRWeb (prweb.com) or to an RSS online generator like the one found at RSS Specifications (rss-specifications.com/rss-submission.htm).

➡ *Link exchange directories*. Participating with a link exchange program works pretty much like reciprocal links. Just make sure to use niche directories that specifically relate to your business. This should be a carefully done process that is hands-on. In other words, don't use an automatic submission program.

➡ *Give away freebies*. Offer visitors a free e-book, report, software, or other type of product from your website. Other sites often link back to sites offering freebies if they think their visitors or subscribers would benefit.

➡ *Ask*. Look at who your competitors are linking to and see if that site would be willing to give you a backlink. The worst that will happen is they may say, "No."

➡ *Internal linking*. Be careful to do a thorough job internally linking the pages in your website. If you naturally point to various pages in your site, you will increase your chances of search engines following the links and finding additional pages to index. Periodically test your links. The spiders greatly dislike broken links, which is a sign of sloppy web design.

count that as a strike against you because the site is not relevant to yours, and lower your credibility and ranking. But an incoming link from a women's health or beauty site would definitely be a mark in your favor, and your site will be further elevated if that site ranks higher than yours in search engine results.

Outgoing Links

Relevant outgoing links to other sites play a part in the ranking process with search engines. If you don't have any outgoing links, your site will be considered a dead end, and why would the search engines want to send anyone to a dead end? They want to send visitors to sites that will supply more information, including useful links. By linking to other sites, you are demonstrating your familiarity with a specific topic and that you know enough to recommend other sources of information.

A word of caution when using outgoing links: Don't leave the neighborhood. In other words, if you link to a site that is deemed irrelevant or inappropriate, that is considered a "bad neighborhood" or the "wrong side of the tracks." And the search engines take notice. By linking to a bad site, you are considered a supporter of it and will lose credibility, which drops your ranking.

Always carefully check out a site before linking to it. Not only should that site be complimentary to yours, but it should also be listed in the search engines. If you are still unsure and don't feel comfortable, don't link.

Reciprocal Links

Reciprocal links are text links or banner ads that are swapped with another website owner. This can be done through link exchange programs or by contacting the website owner directly and asking for an exchange. Many sites feature a "favorite links" page with partners they are exchanging links with.

Reciprocal links are better than no links at all, but one-way links (incoming) are the best. Many of the search engines keep track of how many sites point back to your link. The more sites that promote your business, the higher visibility your website will have when someone does a search. If you are trading links with other website owners, just make sure their site is complimentary to yours.

CLICK TIP

Site maps are a very easy way for search engine bots to gather data. Every business website should have a site map to make it easy for visitors and crawlers to access its pages. Use simple text links because crawlers often have trouble reading Java script, drop-down menus, and search boxes.

To start the process, find good quality sites through your preferred search engine and add their link with a brief description to your site. The description is important because it needs to contain at least one keyword that relates to your site. (Note: If you are providing a link through an article, a description is not necessary.) Next, contact the website owner and ask him to reciprocate. Be sure to provide the correct URL and description for your site.

If you have not received a reply within three to four weeks, check the site to see if your link has been added. If not, send a friendly reminder in case your e-mail was lost or overlooked. Wait another couple of weeks and if you still haven't heard anything or don't see your link, remove the other company's without further ado. Keep track of sites you have linked to or requested links from so as not to repeat yourself.

Using Meta Tags

Meta tags are HTML information that is placed in the "head" of your web pages. With the exception of the title tag, this information does not appear on your web page for the viewing public. However, this behind-the-scenes information is what search engines are looking for when they visit your site. The better organized your meta tags are, the easier it is for them to read and the better your placement will be in search results.

→ *Title Tag.* This is the main heading of your web page and it's very important that it accurately reflects the main keywords associated with your site.

➡ *Site Description Tag.* Give a brief one- or two-sentence description of your site that you would like to see placed in search engines' listings next to the title.

➡ *Keyword Tags.* While you need to put all relevant keywords within the content of your site, think of this tag as the reinforcement area. It's generally recommended that you include approximately 25 words or phrases separated by commas.

Although browsers do not display meta tags, you still have the ability to view them with a couple of clicks of the mouse. This can be especially helpful when looking at what your competitors are doing with their sites. Type a few keywords in your browser's search box and select one of the top three results. When you are on the website, click the "View" tab at the top of your browser's screen, and scroll down to "Source." Figure 6.1 demonstrates how that box looks using an Internet Explorer browser. This will bring up the underlying HTML code that makes up that site or page, with the meta tags positioned near the top. In the following example, you can see the meta tags that go in between the opening and closing of the "head," including the title, site description, and keywords:

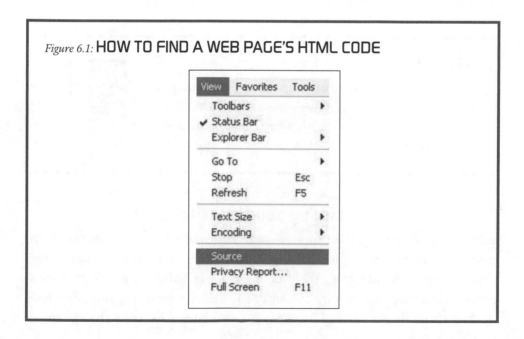

Figure 6.1: **HOW TO FIND A WEB PAGE'S HTML CODE**

```
<HEAD>
<TITLE>Traveling4Business.com—Business Travel, Flights, Hotels,
Cars, Cheap Fares, Great Deals</TITLE>
<META name= "description" content= Great bargains, advice, tips,
and tools for the discerning business traveler.">
<META name= "keywords" content="Traveling for Business,
Traveling4Business.com, traveling4business.com, business travel,
business trip, business traveler, air fare, reservations, business, car
rentals, car reservations, cars, maps, rail, traveler reviews, discount,
travel, jobs, international, domestic, last minute deal, deal, cheap
ticket, credit card, cheap airfare, flights, discount flights, online reser-
vations, destination information, restaurant reviews, travel packages,
travel guides, travel information, travel insurance, hotel, hotel reserva-
tions, lodging, commuter tips, airports, luggage">
</HEAD>
```

Most search engine crawlers are going to pick out the relevant keywords in the content of your web page, but making the best use of meta tags is added insurance those keywords and phrases get noticed.

CLICK TIP

For more information about search engine optimization strategies (including the use of meta tags), visit Search Engine Watch (searchenginewatch.com). It has a firm finger on the pulse of the SEO industry which it shares in helpful tutorials and articles.

Listing Your Website

Search engines make it their number-one goal to discover and index all of the content available on the internet to provide surfers with the best search experience. And the major ones such as Google and Yahoo! use the free crawl process to stay abreast of new and updated sites. Technically, you don't have to do a thing to get noticed by these search engines because the electronic spiders will eventually find you. The question is when? Since you probably don't want to wait for them to find you six months down the road, go ahead and get a head start by submitting your URL to the four major search engines:

1. *Google (google.com)*. This search engine was chosen four times as the Most Outstanding Search Engine by Search Engine Watch (searchengine watch.com) readers. It is also used to provide AOL search results.

2. *Yahoo! (yahoo.com)*. Considered the internet's oldest directory, Yahoo! implements its own crawler-based search technology with specialized search options for browsers.

3. *Live Search (live.com)*. Formerly MSN Search, this search engine has new innovative features including the ability to save searches and have them automatically updated.

4. *Ask (ask.com)*. Formerly AskJeeves.com, there is not a free way to submit your website to this search engine. Unless you are willing to participate in the PPC-based sponsored listing program, you will have to wait for its crawlers to find you.

When you submit your website to one of the major search engines, go ahead and include one or two additional pages along with your home page. Typically, search engines index your other pages by following the links you provide. However, sometimes pages get missed. Therefore, you should submit the top three pages that best represent your entire website. (However, no more than three.) These alternative web pages can also serve you in case your primary index page is not working properly. It is also recommended that you personally submit your site to search engines so you can take note of any problems reported. Entrusting this to a service, or even an automatic submission program, is not the wisest move.

Another often-ignored point is that webmasters should resubmit their site after making major changes to their web pages.

> ## Words of Wisdom
>
> *The two smartest things I've done are learning how to optimize a website, starting with my own, and launching and continuing a regular, free e-mail newsletter for anyone who would care to subscribe.*
>
> —JONATHAN BERNSTEIN, PRESIDENT, BERNSTEIN CRISIS MANAGEMENT, LLC

While search engines revisit sites periodically, some are smart enough to realize that many pages only change once or twice a year. Therefore, a search engine may limit periodic visits to a semi-annual basis. By resubmitting your pages immediately after republishing them, you can help your site to stay current with major search engines—and thus improve in the rankings.

TEN STEPS FOR INCREASING VISIBILITY ONLINE

Jon Rognerud, an e-business columnist for Entrepreneur.com and SEO consultant (jonrognerud.com), feels that most small businesses that run a website today don't have the insider knowledge to optimize their content and overall visibility online. "I personally handle internet marketing issues—SEO, PPC, e-mail marketing, copywriting—every day, and I'm always surprised to see how many businesses have no understanding of what SEO means, let alone know how to approach it," he says. "You need a strong, long-term commitment to SEO and must always stay on top of the search engines and their ever-changing, underlying landscape."

Rognerud offers the following ten-step plan to improve site visibility and increase search-friendliness. The first five steps address parts of your website's HTML code, while the final five are more abstract. Together, they add up to a must-do SEO list:

1. Title tag (<title>SEO Gone Wild—microsaw.com</title>)
   - This is most important of all. If you have the title tag set up right and it's a unique enough phrase, you could rank on page one for this alone.
   - Write your keywords early in the title, and place your company name last—unless you are Coca-Cola, or have a huge brand.

2. Meta tags
   - Description—<meta name="description" content=""/>. Place your page content description between the blank quotes with a call to action statement like, "Sign up here," or "Call us at 800 XXX-XXXX."
   - Keywords—<meta name="keywords" content=""/>. Place keywords between the quotation marks after "content," separated by commas. Google ignores this, but it appears that other search engines still review it.

TEN STEPS FOR INCREASING VISIBILITY ONLINE, CONTINUED

3. Header tags

   - H1—This HTML tag should contain your core keywords, one per page.

   - H2—This HTML tag should contain derivatives of the keywords.

4. Body

   - Content—Use content that matches the keywords on your site. You should ideally have 400 to 800 words on a page.

   - Bolding—Include bolded keywords that match your topic/theme on the page.

   - Create a blog—WordPress (wordpress.com) is an amazing blog that is free and can easily be optimized via plug-ins. Then, write entries twice a week.

5. Linking

   - Use links and anchor text to create popularity and reputation around keywords (example: don't link to just "click here," but create a better link like, "download the digital camera white paper").

   - Internal links (link to other pages on your site).

   - Outbound links (you link to another authority site on your topic).

   - Reciprocal links (join link exchanges and contact partners to exchange links).

   - One-way links (when other sites link to your blog, press releases or articles) are typically more effective than outbound and reciprocal ones.

   - For some internal links, use "rel=nofollow" in the code to avoid losing PageRank to less important pages like "about us," "contact us," and "privacy policy."

6. Domains

   - If starting a new site, try to get an established URL (purchase it if you have to).

   - Use keywords in an easy-to-remember domain. Google recognizes domains that have been around and establishes credibility; you can thus avoid the Google Sandbox (where you don't show up in the index for months, potentially).

TEN STEPS FOR INCREASING VISIBILITY ONLINE, CONTINUED

7. Users first, then search engine

   - Make sure your sites have valuable and readable content. If you've optimized for search engines only and no users stick around your website, you haven't been successful.

   - Navigation, directory structures, and file names should be well defined. An easy way to do this is to use breadcrumb navigation and linked navigation, not flash, JavaScript, or image-based links. Develop a flat directory structure (no more than three levels deep), and name your keywords in the file name (ex: content-management-system.htm).

8. Keyword research

   - Keyword development is one of the first places to start. Two to three keywords per page is possible. Combined with the items listed in the first five steps above, you will have a high success score.

   - Use tools like Yahoo! Search Marketing (sem.smallbusiness.yahoo.com/search enginemarketing), Google's Keyword Tool (adwords.google.com/select/ KeywordToolExternal), and SEO Book Keywords Tool (tools.seobook.com/ keyword-tools/seobook).

   - Try to shoot for keywords that have higher search counts; over 20,000 searches for your keyword are good, but it all depends on your industry.

9. Competition

   - Find out what the competition is doing. Type in your search term into a search engine and locate three to five of the top results. Look at these sites and see what they are doing in the HTML (on-page) and linking (off-page) areas. I'll discuss this later.

   - To find out how many sites are linking to your competition, type "link:http://www.competitorname.com" into Google. Do the same in Yahoo!, and you'll see a higher count because Yahoo! is more all-inclusive.

TEN STEPS FOR INCREASING VISIBILITY ONLINE, CONTINUED

10. Be cool.

- Don't let this business get to you; it's frustrating at times. SEO is a long-term commitment. Some weeks are great, others are not.

- It's a serious investment of time, sweat, and staying the course. The best success factors I've seen: Approach content and website design in a natural way; be ethical (don't spam); and keep it real—it's a business, and nothing comes for free.

Search engine optimization applied correctly will create better visibility online, but always keep in mind it's just one part of your overall marketing strategy.

Chapter 7

Essentials of E-Marketing

*M*any business owners do not enjoy the prospect of marketing, but it can actually be a lot of fun as you devise clever and innovative ways to fill the coffers. To help you do that, the next two chapters provide marketing tips, tricks, and techniques that will encourage clients to take a closer look at your travel services. They also help you identify the competition and how to rise above it.

Whether you're on a shoestring budget or have a boatload to spend on marketing, you've got lots of options. The most important thing to keep in mind about marketing is this: It's not an expense; it's an investment in your business.

The internet has become the number-one place people turn to when researching vacation destinations and purchasing travel packages, according to Peter Geisheker, CEO of The Geisheker Group (geisheker.com). "As an online travel business, you need to do everything you can to make sure when people are searching for the travel destination you specialize in, your website is found," he says.

> ## Words of Wisdom
>
> *A great resource for information on your market is your competition. Go to their websites and sign up for all their newsletters, white papers, technical papers, industry surveys, and conference reports. Get on their e-mail lists.*
>
> —FROM *MADSCAM: KICK-ASS ADVERTISING WITHOUT THE MADISON AVENUE PRICE TAG* BY GEORGE PARKER

The American Marketing Association (marketingpower.com) defines marketing as "the process of planning and executing the conception, pricing, promotion, and distribution of ideas, goods, and services to create exchanges that satisfy individual and organizational goals." This means you have to apply different solutions to different circumstances. There isn't a single marketing technique that fits all. You need to try a variety of strategies such as search engine optimization, pay-per-click ad campaigns, writing articles (one to two per month or more), and sending out at least one news-based press release every month to see which works best for your business.

Developing a Marketing Plan

A well-thought-out marketing plan is essential to the success of your online travel business because it takes you from the brainstorming stage to a profitable operation. Just as each business is different, no two marketing plans are alike. However, most contain the same fundamental elements provided by Jacquelyn Lynn in *The Entrepreneur's Almanac 2008–2009*:

➡ *Define your product or services.* You need to know precisely what your product or service is and what it will do for your customers. Be very specific. Successful marketing requires a solid understanding of the features and benefits of every aspect of your product.

➡ *Identify your customers.* Who will buy your product or service, and why? Again, be specific. Where do these people live and work? How much money do they make? How often will they buy? Understand various buying sensitivities, such as the importance of brand, location, guarantee, and price.

➡ *Identify your competition.* Know your competition as well as yourself. Who else sells what you sell? Where are they? How do they market? How similar are their products or services? What are the comparative advantages between what they do and what you plan to do? What is their pricing structure? What do their customers like and dislike about them? What would make their customers buy from you instead?

You may believe you don't have any direct competition, that is, that no one else in your market is doing exactly what you do. But if that's the case, how do you know there's a need for your business? And how are your prospective customers getting that need met currently?

➡ *Set your prices.* How much you charge affects your profitability and your position in the market. Understand what your costs are, what competitors are charging, and how your price relates to your overall marketing strategy.

➡ *Explain how you will interact with your customers.* This includes the general promotion of your business as well as the actual sales process. How will prospective customers learn about you? What will drive them to you? How will you advertise? Once potential customers become aware of what you have to offer, how will you convert them from prospects to buyers?

Develop a very specific plan and plot it out at least one year in advance. Keep in mind that this is not a linear process. You may begin with a particular product or service only later to realize you can capture a greater share of the market with a few

> **CLICK TIP**
>
> Be sure your web address is printed on your business cards, all your promotional materials, and all your ads. You might also include it in your after-hours voice mail announcement.

adjustments. As you study your competition and move through the learning curve created by a new business venture, new opportunities and ideas may be presented that necessitate changes to your plan.

Article (or Bum) Marketing: Why It's Great for Business!

Article marketing is a low-cost form of advertising in which someone writes a short article related to some aspect of their business, which is then tied into their service or product. Once the article has been written, it's freely distributed online or in print publications. Immediately following the article is an author's biography that includes contact information, references, the name of the business—and most importantly, the site's URL.

These freely distributed articles can expand your credibility within the travel industry and also reap some free publicity. This model of marketing has actually been in existence for decades—as long as there has been any sort of mass printing process. For example, when newspapers and magazines were only available in print, a business owner might write a useful article for the newspaper free of charge. In return, the publication provided the writer's contact information. Since the internet has reconstructed how businesses operate in recent years, the need for article marketing has steadily increased. Many websites are looking for free content, and authors who have products and services to promote can certainly see the benefit in writing free material.

When the article is ready for publication, it's then submitted to popular article websites and directories—unless this task has been passed on to a SEO marketing service. Then website owners and e-zine publishers pick it up and place it on their sites, which helps your site climb up the ranks of the search engines. When prospective customers see the article and identify the author (you) as an authority, they feel comfortable ordering the product or using the service being subtly promoted.

CLICK TIP

Article marketing is affectionately called "bum marketing" because the concept is so simple even a bum off the street could do it.

There are many advantages to this type of online marketing, especially because there is no major investment other than your time, unless you decide to outsource the writing and/or hire a SEO firm to market your articles.

How Search Engine Optimization Ties In

Obviously, the higher ranked an article or page is, the more traffic it will draw. This also means a greater chance of increased sales. One of the most important lessons in learning SEO and getting higher earnings is acquiring more HTML links pointing back to your site from other websites (discussed in detail in Chapter 6). This is why syndicated articles often link back to a business owner's website within the biography box. Having these links is one of the most important ways to improve your search rankings.

Unfortunately, there are problems with article marketing, specifically on the quality of syndicated articles. Many have been poorly written and are a far cry from the syndicated articles that appear in newspapers. Why the low quality? Too often web owners create the article exclusively for SEO purposes, which means that the articles have either been reprinted or stuffed full of keywords without much thought to coherency. Then there are business owners who will write pretty much anything for the sole purpose of submitting the articles to directories in the hopes of gaining recognition.

Some experts speculate that the low quality of articles has resulted from the sudden popularity of article marketing, and thus the rushed production of articles. Others fault writers for poorly researching information or for having no particular experience with a niche subject. These articles may get rapid exposure for a business, but in the end the marketing campaign will be unsuccessful. Web viewers are not stupid and notice if the author has no idea what he is talking about. Therefore, it pays to be informed about the subject you are working with in your article marketing campaign. It may involve producing higher quality work by thoroughly researching a subject or hiring freelance writers to do the job more effectively.

Tips for Approaching an Article Marketing Campaign

I talked about finding your travel niche in Chapter 2 and at the risk of being redundant, I'm going to re-emphasize some things: Start by finding a specific niche market that you can completely explore. Starting too broadly may be setting yourself up for failure, or at least achieving only medium-range results. Finding a targeted niche can help you quickly establish visibility for your business.

Next, look for keyword phrases with low competition to start targeting your audience. When you write your article (or have someone write it for you), optimize the work according to the targeted keyword phrase. If you are outsourcing the writing, finding qualified writers can be difficult. Effective SEO writers must be experienced in writing coherent stories and have skills in working with SEO content and sales writing to make the article engaging to casual surfers.

When submitting your article to popular article directories, remember that your ultimate goal is to provide free content to webmasters and bloggers who appreciate a well-written story and will reprint your article on their blog or website. Mindless linking will not be that valuable in the long run, especially if the articles are of low quality. Remember that one high-quality article is usually more effective than a hundred articles full of gibberish, especially if this one article is posted on a highly-ranked website. In exchange for quality traffic, article marketing need not be "bum marketing"—not if you have something important to share with the world, along with your contact information, of course.

Some popular article directories are:

➡ A1 Articles—a1articles.com
➡ Article Dashboard—articledashboard.com
➡ Author Connection—authorconnection.com/
➡ e-Topic—e-topic.com
➡ Ezine Articles—ezinearticles.com/
➡ GoArticles—goarticles.com
➡ HubPages—hubpages.com
➡ Idea Marketers—ideamarketers.com
➡ iSnare—isnare.com
➡ Search Warp—searchwarp.com
➡ Squidoo—squidoo.com
➡ WikiHow—wikihow.com

Google AdWords: What They Are and How to Use Them

Google is not only one of the biggest and most widely used search engines in the world; it is also one of the most lucrative means of advertising in any medium. Like the other search engines, Google tries to keep the competition fair by showing favoritism toward websites that provide thoroughly original content, relevant keywords, and massive linking with other sites. However, guaranteeing a number-one ranking on a Google search can be difficult because many different factors come into play. To give website owners a different advantage, paid placements are offered as an alternative. Basically, every major search engine accepts paid listings, which are usually marked "Sponsored Links."

Google AdWords are keyword generated text ads. They have been proven to be a very effective form of online advertising because they have a much higher click-through-rate (CTR) than the flashy, colorful banner ads. Most internet users suffer from a condition called "banner blindness." They refuse to be distracted from their primary objective to seek and find; therefore banners are often ignored. Text ads on the other hand are outperforming banner ads five to one because they are specifically targeting the browser who is searching for something in particular, plus they are easy and relatively inexpensive to implement.

Although the technology is new, the concept is not because it harkens back to the old-fashioned way of advertising when companies outbid one another for the opportunity to show a commercial on television. This is essentially what Google AdWords represents: a pay-per-click (PPC) system of advertising technology with participants bidding on select keywords and phrases. When a potential customer types specific keywords into a Google search engine, relevant text ads (known as "contextual advertisement links") appear either on the side or above the natural search results.

The advantages of using Google AdWords are many. Your specialty travel

> ## Words of Wisdom
>
> *The customers have two choices; they can go to somebody else, or they can come to you. You've got to understand what is going to make them come to you.*
>
> —IMRAN AZHAR, CO-FOUNDER, AZHAR THERAPY & FITNESS, OKLAHOMA CITY, OKLAHOMA

website will be separated from the common results page and will reach local customers, as well as national and even worldwide audiences. The disadvantages of using this feature lie mainly in the limitations. The biggest limitation is that you can only write short blurbs about your product or service, typically one or two sentences.

What Determines the Order of Paid Listings?

Theoretically, your ad is placed in accordance with how much you are willing to pay for each click. However, Google has taken the process a step further by taking into account the number of times an ad impression that has been generated by a particular keyword or phrase is clicked, in addition to the amount an advertiser is willing to pay. So even if you paid less than Daddy Warbucks for a keyword but your ad generated more clicks, you could go to the front of the line and have your ad promoted ahead of his.

The determining factor is the overall quality score. This is calculated through historical click-through rates as well as the relevance of the website's ad according to text phrase. Therefore, while this system is largely money-based, there are still guidelines to be followed. After all, Google gets paid every time a web surfer clicks on one of the ads, so they want to insure a strong click-through rate.

It should also be understood that impressions are free. The term "impression" means whenever a surfer sees your advertisement. No matter how many times your AdWord appears on a website or search results page, you are not charged anything until it is clicked. Of course, the objective is to encourage potential customers to click your ads as often as possible. If your advertising campaign fails to attract a moderate to high quantity of clicks, then Google will lose money and possibly deactivate your keywords.

Dane Steele Green (steeletravel.com) uses an AdWord campaign for his website with great success. His strategy is using his competitors as keywords and phrases. "Put your competitors in your Google AdWords," Green recommends. "That's where you'll get your clicks. If people are looking specifically for you, they already know what to look for. But if they are looking for one of your competitors, your ad will pop up and you just might steal one of their customers."

Remember when you use Google AdWords, your intent is not merely to get impressions or even direct links to your website. Your objective is to sell your product or service, therefore justifying the expense of using Google AdWords. This can be done by giving browsers a strong call to action in your short, limited blurb.

Google has made internet advertising not only easy, but also very affordable to the average consumer who is new to the internet and does not have a large amount of capital to invest in marketing. Make a little money for Google, and the world's most popular search engine can make a little more money for you.

The Benefits of Social Networking

It's true that "time is money," and time spent networking online is critical to the success of your online business. This is a low- or no-cost marketing strategy that can have a global impact while building personal relationships and credibility. Many online businesses have joined this growing trend and are promoting themselves via social networks like MySpace (myspace.com), Facebook (facebook.com), and LinkedIn (linkedin.com). It's not at all unusual for one entrepreneur to ask another, "Do you twitter?" while referring to the wildly popular micro-blogging service (twitter.com) that allows members to send short updates or "tweets" to other users.

James Hills (mantripping.com) says that social networking sites are a great way to get your content indexed fast. "They provide a conduit for visitors to come to your site and are very quick to show results," he says. Hills

---

CLICK TIP

One of the best ways to promote your business in e-mails and on discussion boards is by providing direct links in your signature line. This simple marketing technique works as an unobtrusive promotional pitch, almost like a virtual business card. Keep it short with no more than two to three lines that include a link to your website or affiliate landing page.

---

recommends networking sites like Propeller (propeller.com), Digg (digg.com), MySpace (myspace.com), and StumbleUpon (stumbleupon.com) to help with site promotion.

Another advantage of social networking sites is that you can build profiles to enhance your visibility and link back to your website. Participating on the more popular networking sites will provide the best search results when others are looking for you, which makes them great resources for maximizing cross-promotion for your business.

Other types of online communities that have been around since the 1990s are listservs (e-mail distribution lists), discussion forms, newsgroups, bulletin boards, and chat rooms. These still provide great opportunities to become known as an expert in your niche and drive traffic to your website. Google, Yahoo!, and AOL all have special interest groups that millions of people regularly interact on. Also, many organizations related to the travel industry (see Appendix) have discussion forums that members can network on.

> ### Words of Wisdom
>
> *Talent is cheaper than table salt. What separates the talented individual from the successful one is a lot of hard work.*
>
> —STEPHEN KING, AUTHOR

Beth Whitman (wanderlustandlipstick.com) uses social networking as a big part of her site optimization strategy, including participating on the various networking sites and discussion forums. "It's all about befriending people and getting to know them through these various sites," she says. "The whole social networking aspect can be time consuming, but done consistently it can be very effective."

Get Involved

Whenever using any type of social network, forum, or newsgroup, it's important to become an active participant. When joining a community, send in an introductory e-mail telling the other members who you are and what you do. Keep it brief and make sure to include your contact information, especially your website, in the signature line.

Get involved in conversations by asking questions or contributing to topics you can answer with authority. Just be careful not to become a powerhouse

ONLINE GIFT CERTIFICATES

Gift certificates can work as a customer reward and retention tool as well as a way to acquire new customers. For example, you may set up a rewards program and give a gift certificate of $5 for every $100 your customers spend on your website during a specified time period. You can also encourage existing customers to buy gift certificates as presents.

Assign a code number to each certificate and keep track of the name of the customer, date of purchase, amount, and when the certificate was redeemed. Though buyers generally like to have a physical certificate, you don't need to require that they send you that piece of paper to redeem the certificate; they can do it with their code number when they make a purchase.

There are several gift certificate templates available online at sites such as Giftcard Designer (giftcarddesigner.com) or Certificate Wizard (certificatewizard.com), or you can create your own using MS Word, Printmaster, or similar software. When you issue a certificate, complete the form then scan and save it as a .JPG or .PDF file so it cannot be tampered with. You can e-mail the file or mail a hard copy to your customer.

and dominate all of the conversations with your expertise. This can be a real turn-off, and the other members will soon tune you out. Find your balance and respond with helpful tips and sage advice when appropriate. It won't take long before other members recognize you as a specialist and start deferring to you while taking a closer look at your business.

Set aside a specific time each day to participate on relevant discussion forums and newsgroups so that you are not easily sidetracked. The biggest investment will be your time, so you don't want to waste it.

Online Newsletters

It's a fact: online newsletters (aka e-zines) can further your marketing goals and get your message out to current and prospective customers in a cost-effective, credible manner. Interested parties subscribe to receive articles and informative tips from you, and it puts your business's name in front of them on a regular basis.

Newsletters are an effective way to legitimately capture the names and e-mails of prospective customers, so this is an important marketing tool. Once this information is entered into your database, you can offer promotions, insider information, free trials, monthly contests, and more. Dane Steele Green (steeletravel.com) currently has 5,000 subscribers for his bi-monthly newsletter, with more people signing up every day. People "opt-in" by clicking the newsletter link on the main page of the website, which gives Green the opportunity to promote upcoming excursions way in advance. "Some people book a year in advance, while others wait until a couple of days before we leave," he says. "The newsletters help keep the information fresh in their minds without being obtrusive."

Entice new subscribers by offering a bonus such as a travel guide or e-book. Retain subscribers by holding monthly drawings for prizes (ideally a promotional item that matches your product line) and providing great articles. The content does not have to be lengthy, but it should be solid and relevant. If you send your subscribers junk, they'll unsubscribe, and you'll lose a captive audience. Green plans to add more subscribers to his mailing list by promoting sweepstakes for free trips.

Provide short, interesting articles and subtly weave in a powerful marketing message. Include checklists and tests that encourage reader interaction.

WARNING

With just a few keystrokes you can find hundreds of websites selling e-mail addresses by the thousands. While the temptation to quickly build up your customer database is great, don't do it.
These e-mail addresses are usually "harvested" and in noncompliance with the CAN-SPAM Act (see page 108). The only e-mail addresses you should have in your database are the ones who have "opted-in" of their own free will.

Quote experts, including experts from the travel industry, to make your point, but it's generally not acceptable to sell your service in the text of the article. Use a separate ad for your sales message. You can also include affiliate links and classified ads from third-party sponsors in your newsletter.

If your newsletter offers readers information they can use, you'll get maximum readership. By educating customers and prospective clients about important travel issues, you help to make them better consumers who are more likely to buy from you because they understand the value you offer. Finally, you are positioning yourself as an expert in the travel industry, which builds credibility.

E-zines need to be sent out often enough to keep your customers interested and not so often that you annoy them. Let your customers know when they sign up how often they can expect to hear from you. For example, Green sends out his newsletters once every two weeks.

Just as you need a privacy policy for your website, you also need one for the mailing lists you develop. Include a statement on your subscription invitation that says something like: "We value your privacy and do not take your trust for granted. We will never sell, share, or lease your name, e-mail address, or other information with anyone." Each newsletter you send should have a link to allow the recipient to unsubscribe.

Though it's possible to manage an e-mail list manually, it's far more efficient to automate through an autoresponder service. Many are free through discussion list forums such as Yahoo Groups or Topica. Others are available

CLICK TIP

Shorten lengthy hyperlinks in newsletters and other publications by using TinyURL (tinyurl.com) or Snipr (snipr.com). For example, an extended affiliate link can be significantly reduced from 130+ characters to 22, while disguising the fact that it's an affiliate link. These free services not only reduce the length of a URL, but can also help you manage your links by monitoring how many unique clicks they receive.

through monthly subscription services such as Constant Contact (constant contact.com) or Aweber (aweber.com) that come with professional templates, HTML features, and are ad-free.

The Secrets of Automatic Marketing with Autoresponders

It's been said that customers need to hear your name at least seven times before they buy from you. Autoresponders make it easy to ensure that they do. Essentially an autoresponder is a computer program that automatically answers e-mail messages sent to it with one, or several, responses, according to the e-mail address it's sent to. For example, if you have a web address at mycompany.com, you could set up your autoresponder to reply to e-mail messages sent to special e-mail addresses you've set up, like subscribe@ mycompany.com, info@mycompany.com, or newsletter@mycompany.com.

Most web hosts include autoresponder-type packages with their services; however, in these days of overwhelming spam, it's often more effective to use a professional autoresponder service, such as Aweber.com or GetResponse .com. This improves your ability to ensure delivery, manage large lists of e-mail addresses, and avoid accusations of spam.

What Can You Use Autoresponders For?

Use autoresponders to send out automatic responses to support queries, to send out price lists; for e-mail newsletters, for marketing follow-ups, for online courses. An autoresponder's uses are limited only by your needs.

Safe Ways to Obtain Leads for Your Autoresponders

Options for obtaining leads for your autoresponders include opt-in forms on your website and by advertising. You could also use mailing lists you currently have, adding all the leads to a particular autoresponder. However, be careful with this approach. Make sure that the people on your lists have requested information from you. If they haven't asked for the information you're sending them and if you have no proof that they asked, you may be accused of sending spam.

Spam accusations can have serious consequences. Your messages may be blocked by large internet service providers like AOL and EarthLink, and even more seriously, you may find that your web hosting company removes your website from the web. You also run the risk of customers filing lawsuits.

Avoid Accusations of Spam with Double Opt-in

An easy way to avoid spam accusations with an autoresponder is to use a process called "double opt-in." This means prospective customers have to sign up for your information, which gives you proof via the IP address of the computer they're using, as well as respond to a verification message, confirming that they're willing to receive information. This provides you with the defense you need should you be accused of spamming.

Enhance Open-Rates for Your Autoresponder

In *The Entrepreneur's Almanac 2008–2009* (Entrepreneur Media, 2007), by Jacquelyn Lynn, readers are advised to make the subject lines of autoresponder messages compelling, while avoiding words that can trigger spam filters. "If you're sending a newsletter, your subject line should clearly state the name of the newsletter so the recipient can easily identify it," the author advises. "Commercial autoresponder packages allow you to track clicks on hyperlinks in your messages so you can measure response rates."

Autoresponders are an excellent marketing tool, because they can work for you 24/7/365, with little expense. They can extend your marketing reach, and used with care, they build your company's brand and bottom line.

CLICK TIP

Sign up for Google Alerts (google.com/alerts) to find out who is talking about you and your business online. This handy service also helps you keep tabs on a competitor or get the latest news and events on a particular topic. Dane Steele Green (steeletravel.com) has been delighted to find his company's press releases all over the web.

The CAN-SPAM Act:
Requirements for Commercial E-Mailers

The CAN-SPAM Act of 2003 (Controlling the Assault of Non-Solicited Pornography and Marketing Act) has specific rules and guidelines for anyone sending out commercial e-mails. Spammers are subject to severe consequences if they violate the law, which became effective January 1, 2004. The nation's consumer protection agency, the Federal Trade Commission (FTC), has the authority to enforce the CAN-SPAM Act, along with the Department of Justice (DOJ). Other federal and state agencies can enforce the law against organizations under their jurisdiction, and companies that provide internet access may sue violators, as well.

Here's a rundown of the law's main provisions taken from the FTC website (ftc.gov/bcp/conline/pubs/buspubs/canspam.shtm):

➡ It bans false or misleading header information. Your e-mail's "From," "To," and routing information, including originating domain name and e-mail address, must be accurate and identify the person who initiated the e-mail.

➡ It prohibits deceptive subject lines. The subject line cannot mislead the recipient about the contents or subject matter of the message.

➡ It requires that your e-mail give recipients an opt-out method. You must provide a return e-mail address or another internet-based response mechanism that allows a recipient to ask you not to send future e-mail messages to that e-mail address, and you must honor the requests. You may create a menu of choices to allow a recipient to opt out of certain types of messages, but you must include the option to end any commercial messages from the sender.

Any opt-out mechanism you offer must be able to process opt-out requests for at least 30 days after you send your commercial e-mail. When you receive an opt-out request, the law gives you ten business days to stop sending e-mail to the requestor's e-mail address. You cannot help another entity send e-mail to that address, or have another entity send e-mail on your behalf to that address. Finally, it's illegal for you to sell or transfer the e-mail addresses of people who choose not to receive your e-mail, even in the form of a mailing list, unless you transfer the addresses so another entity can comply with the law.

➡ It requires that commercial e-mail be identified as an advertisement and include the sender's valid physical postal address. Your message must contain clear and conspicuous notice that the message is an advertisement or solicitation and that the recipient can opt out of receiving more commercial e-mail from you. It also must include your valid physical postal address.

Penalties are steep; each violation is subject to fines of up to $11,000. Additional fines can be levied against people who "harvest" e-mail addresses from websites or other online services; who produce e-mail addresses at random by combining names, letters, or numbers into different variations; who try to register for multiple e-mail addresses for the sole purpose of spamming; or who take advantage of open relays or proxies to send out unauthorized e-mails (more on that in Chapter 11). In addition to fines, the DOJ can seek criminal punishment that may include imprisonment.

For more information on the CAN-SPAM Act, go to the FTC website: ftc.gov/bcp/conline/pubs/buspubs/canspam.shtm.

ALERT THE MEDIA

Press releases are free publicity spots that expose your business to the community; but to be printed in the news the information has to be newsworthy. One way to use this subtle form of self-promotion is to tie the announcement to local or national events, community programs, or holidays.

Peter Geisheker, CEO of The Geisheker Group (geisheker.com) suggests writing press releases on exciting news about traveling to the destination you specialize in, such as why traveling to Mexico makes a great family vacation or the secret beaches of Mexico. Or if you have done something special such as making it far easier or safer for people to travel by using your services, write a press release. "When you write a

ALERT THE MEDIA, CONTINUED

SAMPLE PRESS RELEASE

FOR IMMEDIATE RELEASE

Press Contact:
Dane Steele Green
info@steeletravel.com
646-688-2274

Steele Luxury Travel Launches
Company Offers Indulgent 5-Star Vacationing for Gays and Lesbians

14 March 2008, New York, NY - Every year over 1 million discerning gays and lesbians travel abroad, accounting for over 10 percent of the overall travel market. Many gay travel companies have emerged, but none cater to the affluent gay and lesbian customer. Aware of this gaping need in the marketplace, travel expert Dane Steele Green is launching **Steele Luxury Travel**, a new company offering the ultimate 5 star luxury vacation packages to leading gay destinations worldwide.

The new breed of globetrotting gays seek nightlife, culture, cuisine and demand luxury accommodations and services. The destination cities offered by Steele Luxury Travel are popular among this set for their famous Gay pride celebrations and world renowned cultural events.

For each vacation destination, Steele Travel guests experience the ultimate in chic, first-class style. Lodging is always in a 5-star hotel with complimentary daily breakfast, transportation to and from the airport and within destination cities is via Mercedes-Benz chauffeur service. Even the flights are a pleasure, as guests fly only in premium business-class cabins, with large, comfortable recliners that lie back as far as 180 degrees.

Do you have the desire to take private tango lessons in the heart of Buenos Aires? How about a helicopter tour of Rio de Janeiro? Good news! Steele Travel packages are fully customizable; guests plan their vacations exactly as they wish, and the company's experienced travel experts cater to every detail. "Steele Luxury Travel pampers travelers with amenities and services that go far beyond first class," said Green. "Our goal is for every guest to arrive at their destination feeling pampered and relaxed."

Currently, Steele Luxury Travel offers five vacation packages to four gay-friendly destinations:
- *Buenos Aires Gay Pride:* November 6 – November 13, 2008
- *Rio de Janeiro Reveillon 2009:* December 26, 2008 – January 4, 2009
- *Rio de Janeiro Carnival:* February 17 – February 24, 2009
- *São Paulo Gay Pride:* June 2009
- *Mykonos Island Escape:* August 2009

Steele Luxury Travel is a new concept designed to offer the seasoned globetrotter a unique life experience by providing personalized itineraries to various gay event destinations worldwide. Steele Luxury Travel not only provides you with an extraordinary vacation; we deliver your international fantasy. For more information please visit: **www.SteeleTravel.com**.

(Reprinted with permission courtesy of Dane Steele Green, www.steeletravel.com)

ALERT THE MEDIA, CONTINUED

press release, think of it as a new story to excite the media into wanting to contact you and interview you for articles, kind of like a news teaser," he says. "Press releases are a great way to get free publicity and to make yourself viewed as a top expert in your field." Geisheker also says one of the best places to post your press releases is PRWeb (prweb.com). "I recommend posting at least one press release per month," he says. "You should also fax your press release to travel magazines." For more information on how to write a great press release, go to The Publicity Hound (publicityhound.com).

Make up a list of media contacts, including television, radio, newspaper, and community organizations so that when you are ready, you can send out a press release blitz. Be sure to include your contact information, including your cell phone number. Folks in the media work on tight deadlines. If they can't reach you right away to ask questions, they may be inclined to drop the story and move on.

Chapter 8

Marketing Your Business Offline

*I*t's just as important to promote your business offline as it is online. Believe it or not, there are still quite a few potential customers who do not use the internet at all, while others are just casual browsers who do not have a lot of expertise surfing the web. A lot of focus is given to internet marketing to promote businesses, but you should also know that there are many different types of offline marketing strategies that you can use to great advantage. For maximum benefits and better exposure, integrate both traditional and online marketing efforts.

Network, Network, Network!

Word-of-mouth will ultimately be your best and most reliable source for promoting your online travel business. Tell everyone about your new venture—that includes family, friends, co-workers, business associates, neighbors, church members, and members of any civic, professional, or fraternal organizations you belong to. Develop relationships with anyone you can think of who comes into regular contact with your target market. For instance, if you specialize in honeymoon packages, get to know bridal shop owners and wedding planners in your area so they will recommend your website. Reciprocate by endorsing their services to brides who look you up or placing their website link on your site.

Convention and visitors bureaus can also be great places with which to establish relationships. If they can list your business or refer business to you, that is a big plus.

Join Professional Associations

Join local associations, organizations, and civic clubs, especially those affiliated with the travel industry or any other business communities with which you can share information, resources, and services. For example, the Outside Sales Support Network (ossn.com) offers educational programs and networking

---

CLICK TIP

Have your logo and website address imprinted on novelty items such as pens, pencils, cups, or mouse pads to be freely given away to targeted markets. For example, if you have a business travel site, give a pack of pens or some mouse pads to a corporate office. Visit Café Press (cafepress.com) for a wide variety of customizable merchandise.

---

opportunities along with lists of host agencies and travel suppliers, travel discounts, courses for accreditation, merchant credit card service, and much more.

Find out when your local chamber of commerce, Rotary Club, or Toastmasters group holds meetings that you can attend and exchange business cards with new acquaintances. There is a wealth of information you can learn from small-business owners in other industries who have successfully carved out a niche for themselves. James Hills (mantripping.com) says, "You can't beat your local chamber of commerce for building your business. Some chambers are better than others, but for a couple hundred bucks you get access to tons of activities and opportunities to promote yourself."

Jenny Reed (ourcruiseplanners.com) actively belongs to two local networking groups, one of which is the local chapter of the American Business Women's Association (abwa.org). "As a businesswoman, I have learned over the years that you never know when you're going to meet someone who needs your services, or knows someone else who does," she says. "Never underestimate the power of a connection."

Get on Your Soap Box

Hit the "rubber chicken circuit" and make yourself available as a speaker to every professional, fraternal, and service organization in town. Many of these groups meet weekly, and they are always looking for speakers. You may not get paid, but you'll get a free meal, make some valuable contacts, and get the word out about your business.

Develop a 15- to 20-minute presentation about an aspect of the services your business provides, such as setting up tours and planning vacation packages. You may even want to include a PowerPoint slideshow with images of exotic destinations. Keep the information you provide helpful but general— don't make this a sales pitch for your business. Have business cards and brochures or some other useful handout to distribute at the end of your presentation.

Get a list of all the organizations that might be receptive to having you speak and send a letter introducing yourself and offering your services. Some examples are:

- ➡ Kiwanis Club
- ➡ Garden clubs
- ➡ 4-H clubs
- ➡ Nature clubs
- ➡ AAA or church events
- ➡ Theater groups

The chamber of commerce or public library can provide you with a more comprehensive list of networking opportunities within the community.

Advertising and Public Relations

Advertising and public relations are the two key ways you'll promote your business to the public. Where and how you choose to advertise will depend on your budget and your goals.

Direct Mailing

Because of the ability to target well-defined geographical areas, direct mail can sometimes be an effective way to promote your travel business. It also allows you to send a personalized sales message. Several of the entrepreneurs interviewed for this book find that direct mail, whether catalog, letter, flier, or coupon, is an efficient way of targeting customers.

Al DiGuido, CEO of Zeta Interactive (zetainteractive.com), a leading provider of integrated interactive services, says that direct mail can be effective in driving awareness to your website on a local level—at least initially. However, it can be very costly on a sustained basis.

There is no magic formula when using direct mail, except that using a solo mailer is more successful than including your information in a cooperative mailer full of supermarket coupons. Depending on what your services are, you can send a flashy postcard, informative brochure, or a sales letter with a personal touch.

CLICK TIP

Have your business logo imprinted on colorful stickers to be freely handed out or posted around town. Stickers can be placed in a variety of places including outgoing correspondence, community bulletin boards, backpacks, luggage, etc.

MAKE CONTACT WITH COUPONS

If you're not feeling altogether flush, a viable direct-mail alternative is a coupon mailer that groups retail businesses within a community together in a bound coupon book, which usually includes advertisements, discounts, and special offers. The books are mailed nonselectively to all homes within a specific zip code. They aren't as targeted as a direct-mail piece that you'd design yourself, but they can still have great pull. As a business owner, you pay a fee to the company producing and distributing the coupon books; these companies should be listed in your Yellow Pages.

Mailing lists can be purchased from list brokers, which you can find in your Yellow Pages under "Advertising—Direct Mail." These lists come in just about every category, and since you've done your marketing homework, you already know the lists you want. The one-time rental fee for these names is between $35 and $50 per thousand, with a minimum rental of 5,000 names. You can get more bang for your buck—or, to borrow those corporate buzzwords, "add value" to your direct mailer—by presenting some sort of bonus offer. Put something in the ad that will draw in new customers: a discount, coupon, or sweepstakes. This can be an excellent way to generate business.

Postcards

Once you have an established mailing list, maintain your visibility by periodically sending out postcards featuring a photo of couples dining on cruise ship or a family outing in the mountains. Write something like "Wish you were here! You could be for less than you think if you take advantage of our Spring discount specials!"

In *Start Your Own Travel Business and More* (Entrepreneur, 2007), Rich Mintzer says postcards get your message across quickly and efficiently. "Even super-rushed, busy, and jangled types who might toss an advertising-suspect envelope will take the time to read a short message on a postcard," he writes.

"Get creative with those mini-mailings and design a piece that will have your prospects itching to read on and find out who it's from."

Postcards can be easily created with desktop publishing software such as Microsoft Publisher (office.microsoft.com/publisher) and using images from clip-art, your digital camera, or your travel supplier (with its permission, of course). Be sure to provide your contact information on the postcard, including your website, so the recipients know how to find your great travel deals.

Yellow Pages

Using directory advertising, such as the Yellow Pages of the local phone book, is a very important marketing tool that is often overlooked. Believe it or not, people actually use these tomes for more than doorstops and birdcage liners. When a prospective customer is looking for specific travel services in the directory, they are an excellent prospect because they could be actively looking for a gay and lesbian tour operator or senior group travel planner.

Placing your listing under the right category is critical. People need to be able to find you. And you will increase the chances of a potential client seeing your business if you insert your listing under multiple headings or categories.

Business Cards

As small as they are, business cards are a powerful marketing tool. Hand out these little gems at every opportunity. Think of them as mini-billboards that tell people who you are, what you do, and how to reach you. Whenever you meet someone—in church, at your kids' school, in the grocery store, waiting in lobbies, at business meetings, or anywhere else—and the subject of what you do for a living comes up, hand over your business card as you describe your company. As a matter of fact, give people two cards—one to keep and one to pass along to someone else.

A quick-print shop can do a nice, affordable job on your business cards and provide a variety of templates to choose from. You can also design and print them yourself on your computer or order them online from companies like Vista Print (vistaprint.com) for a nominal charge.

CHARITABLE DONATIONS: CAUSE-RELATED MARKETING

Offer vacation packages or weekend getaways as charitable donations to live or silent auctions. This technique can be even more effective if an existing client is a member of that charity's organization and can help to promote your business.

Recently, Dane Steele Green (steeletravel.com) donated a travel package for his company's upcoming Buenos Aires excursion to Jeffrey Fashion Cares (jeffreyfashion-cares.com), a high-end luxury boutique in Manhattan. He was thrilled when the package was auctioned off at $9,000 because that money went straight to the charitable organization. Not only did the vacation package fetch a generous profit for the organization, but it also introduced some new clients to Green.

Television/Radio

Television and radio can be effective in your marketing strategy if you're advertising something concrete, like a seasonal promotion or a special event. It also helps if you're advertising locally, where you know potential customers are listening to your chosen station. While these stations only reach very small geographic areas, their programs are specifically designed to appeal to the people in this limited market. When you buy time on a small radio or cable TV station, you're not paying for wasted circulation. Rates are usually reasonable, and you can create your own interesting, affordable ad.

Magazine and Publication Ads

Magazine and publication ads seem to have minimal effectiveness for online business owners. They are sometimes expensive and can be hard to get responses from unless they are carefully crafted with an explicit call to action. That's usually achieved by promoting a specific product, service, or

CLICK TIP

Be sure to ask every client or prospective client how she heard about you so you can track the effectiveness of your marketing efforts.

information. Add an incentive such as a discount if a client contacts you and mentions seeing the advertisement, or include a coupon as part of your display ad.

Use niche publications that match your business. Advertising in local newspapers is another way to create public awareness of your business.

Trade Shows and Conferences

Trade shows and conferences can be a tremendous opportunity for learning—or a huge waste of time. There are two basic styles of shows: exhibitions, where companies set up booths to display their products and services, and educational conferences, which consist of training sessions in a variety of formats. Many show sponsors combine the two formats for a broader appeal.

Consumer shows focus on home, garden, travel, and other consumer themes, and are typically designed to appeal to the general public. Business-to-business shows are opportunities for exhibitors to market specific products and services to other companies. You can probably benefit from attending both, and in exhibiting in shows that target specific demographics such as seniors, students, or women. Local consumer shows can provide a tremendous amount of exposure at a comparatively affordable cost.

To find about local trade shows in your area, call your local chamber of commerce or convention center and ask for a calendar. You can also check out *Trade Show Week Directory*, which should be available in your public library or online at tradeshowweek.com.

When you've identified potential shows, contact the sponsor for details. Find out who will attend—show sponsors should be able to estimate the total number of attendees and give you demographics so you can tell if they fit your target market profile.

Attend several shows before you exhibit to get a solid sense of how they work and how you can best benefit from them. Once you make the decision to exhibit, choose the show carefully and give careful thought to the setup of your booth. Your exhibit does not need to be elaborate or expensive, but it does need to be professional and inviting. Even though the show sponsors may provide one, do not put a table across the front of your exhibit space; that

---

CLICK TIP

Become a walking ad by having T-shirts, hats, and other accoutrements imprinted with your business name and logo. If you live in a tourist-heavy area and parade around in a trendy shirt or snappy hat, people will take notice. Start with small enough quantities so as not to break the piggybank and distribute them to family and friends, and eventually the general public.

---

creates a visual and psychological barrier that will discourage visitors from coming in. Consider an interactive demonstration that will encourage people to stop for more information. For example, a cruise planner could have information about the latest "floating city" ships with some fun and interesting trivia highlighting facts such as the staggering amount of food they carry per voyage or the number of staff members they need to make each cruise an enjoyable one.

Your signage should focus on the problems you solve for clients, then list your business name. For example, if you operate a senior travel business, the prominent words on your sign might be "Come Sail Away With Us!" and then your company's name.

Arrange for sufficient staffing so you never leave your booth unattended during exhibit hours. You don't want to miss out on even one sales opportunity. Also, it is easy for someone to walk off with valuable items if you're not there.

Consider a giveaway item such as pens, mugs, or notepads imprinted with your company name. Don't display these items openly; doing so will only crowd your booth with "trade show tourists" who are not really prospective clients. Instead, store them discretely out of sight, and present them individually when appropriate. Be sure you have an adequate stock of brochures, business cards, and perhaps discount coupons or a special offer for show attendees.

Chapter 9

Blog Your Way to Success

*T*he history of blogging can be traced back to the 1990s when the internet was in its infancy. "Web logs" began as websites that published running archives of dated entries, and eventually morphed into "blogs. "Blog writing was once associated with academic reports and personal online diaries (and is still frequently used for such purposes), but more often it now carries a professional connotation, such as business writing written by an expert. Blogs may be full-length articles, "microblogs" consisting of a few quotes, or even original graphics and video.

So how do you go about writing a business blog? These types of blogs usually provide news or relevant commentary on a particular subject, such as travel. It also involves learning the basic mechanics of journalism because bloggers spend time researching an issue before reporting on it to their readership. However, because blogging is largely an opinion-based medium, writers have the freedom of expressing more candid viewpoints than traditional journalism would allow using an "editorial" style.

The top seven reasons you need to start blogging for business are:

1. *People often underestimate the power of a blog.* First, consider that you are slowly but surely building a community. If your blog is interesting, people will bookmark your site and visit it regularly. Building a community gives you an audience to whom you can promote your business, share your knowledge or expertise, and soft-sell products and services.

2. *Consider the convenience of having a blog.* You simply log in and broadcast your posts with just a few clicks of a button and you're done. This eliminates the need to hire a web designer and saves a considerable amount of time when it comes to publishing your content. James Hills (mantripping.com) says for a quick startup idea, you really can't go faster and cheaper than a blog. "Go to WordPress.com and set up a simple blog, throw some AdSense ads on it, and start writing," he says.

CLICK TIP

According to recent stats posted on Blog World Expo (blogworld expo.com), more than 147 million Americans use the internet and 57 million regularly read blogs. Over 12 million American adults currently maintain a blog, but only 1.7 million list making money as one of the reasons they blog. As you can see, there is a lot of opportunity for your blogging business to grow.

"To make it work as a business though, you've got to do some research and provide an answer to 'why should anyone care about your blog.' Virtually every topic has been covered, so figure out what your niche is."

3. *You can improve your search engine rankings using a blog.* The cost of generating traffic from search engine marketing (SEM) is actually much lower than other mediums, making business blogging a much more affordable solution. As I discussed in Chapter 6, the search engine ranking of a website is partially based on link popularity and regular content that is easy to index. Blogging makes the process easy so that you can focus on creating new content.

4. *Blogging provides better communications between you and your readers.* On a conventional website users will not know that you have updated its content unless they check back on their own. But a blog automatically informs your subscribers new content is available.

5. *Blogging lets you build brand-awareness with visitors.* Brand-awareness involves building customer awareness of your service or product, as well as communicating your business's message. It takes time to earn customer loyalty, which may also mean having to make monetary investments through ad networking campaigns in order to reap the benefits of long-term probability.

6. *Regular blogging gives you the opportunity to differentiate yourself.* You can separate yourself from the competition, exploit any niches, manage your own professional reputation, and position yourself as an authority in your field.

7. *Networking through blogging is always an important part of business.* It helps you make new contacts, discover new ideas for your business, and get pertinent news and information ahead of the mainstream press. You can even study your target audience by reading the comments of your own visitors or visitors on other blogs.

Blogging is a great way to market your products and services. Never underestimate the value of free publicity. Nor should you ever underestimate the capacity of one small blog that has the potential to grow into a moderate, or even wildly successful venture. Maintaining a blog indicates you care about your business and you are willing to do something for others—such as provide free information or expert opinions—before you sell them a great idea.

Start by filling your archives with well-researched, well-written posts. Keep them relatively short because the typical web reader has a short attention span: more than 200 words per post, but less than 1,000. By keeping the messages short, you can expand on that particular topic in the next post, which increases the quantity and builds up your archives.

Planning Your Blog

Many people understand what a blog is and how to post on one; however, not everyone understands the benefits that blogging can reap. They may blog a few times only to be disappointed because no comments have been left and very little web traffic has been reported. Starting a new blog takes persistence and a dedication to your chosen topic.

Start by drafting a plan for your blog, pretty much in the same way you would a website plan. A well-thought-out plan provides added assurance that your blog will reach its full potential. The main components of your blog plan should be:

➡ *Goal.* What is the main purpose of your blog? Do you want to educate people about certain aspects of the travel industry such as cruising or business? Perhaps you have a product(s) or service that you want to sell. Are you trying to build a community around your passion for mountain biking? Or is this blog designed to be a revenue generator using AdSense and other affiliate links? Beth Whitman (wanderlustandlipstick.com) had dual purposes for creating her blog. The first was to establish herself as an expert in the field of women's travel, and the second was to promote her book, *Wanderlust and Lipstick: The Essential Guide for Women Traveling Solo.*

➡ *Niche.* Chapter 2 discussed the importance of finding your niche. Those same strategies apply to creating and maintaining a blog. Your chosen topic needs to be one that you have an interest in and more-than-a-little familiarity with in order to establish yourself as a credible blogger. You are giving them the benefit of your expertise, so be prepared to dazzle your readers!

- *Competition*. Identify who your competitors are within your selected niche. This will also give you the opportunity to find out how saturated the market is for this particular topic. If it's overcrowded or extremely well-covered, you may need to readjust your tactics. Every topic has unexplored niches, so don't be afraid to venture into unknown territory. Pinpointing your competition can also help you discover what is successful for other bloggers and what isn't. Copy what works and improve on what doesn't.

- *Audience*. Who is your targeted reader, and why would they want to read your blog out of the 114 million other blogs on the internet? What information can you give them that will keep them coming back for more? Knowing what your potential audience wants is the key to providing quality content.

- *Strategy*. Map out timelines to reach specific goals. For example, schedule how many times a day or week you will publish on your blog. Whitman's blog times are every Monday, Wednesday, and Friday morning, while Sue Freeman posts at least once a day—sometimes more. Next, decide how to implement increased traffic goals by

CLICK TIP

Avoid "shotgun" blogging where you are just sending out quick blasts for the sake of updating your blog. Professional bloggers set aside a time each day or week to specifically write informative, quality articles for their blogs. If you don't give your blog the time and attention it deserves, it will quickly dry up and fizzle out.

writing articles for directories or participating on social networks and forums.

➡ *Don't give up!* While a handful of bloggers find sudden online fame, the majority have to work hard at making their blogs a success. "I don't think people realize when they get into it how time consuming it can really be," says Whitman. Commit yourself to the long haul and constantly tweak your plan until you find the perfect formula—and then be prepared to tweak it again. The blogosphere is constantly evolving and changing, so don't be afraid to take risks.

Setting Up Your Blog

Now it's time to talk about the logistics of setting up a blog and how to publish it. There are a lot of options—too many to cover here—so we're just going to provide the basics. However, if you are serious about blogging, we highly recommend that you read J. S. McDougall's *Start Your Own Blogging Business* (Entrepreneur 2007). Not only is it entertaining, but it's very insightful with a ton of information that looks deep into the world of blogging. Using one of McDougall's words, it's "blogtastic!"

Give this Blog a Name

The importance of naming your business and website was discussed in Chapter 4, and those same guidelines apply to naming your blog. The name should be descriptive, memorable, and catchy. When people see or hear it, they should immediately know what topic your blog covers. The same rules also apply to selecting your blog's domain name: keep it short and as close to your blog's name as possible. The ideal scenario is to interlock the names of your online travel website with your blog and domain. For example:

➡ Traveling for Business (Business Name)
➡ traveling4business.com (Website)
➡ traveling4businessblog.com (Blog)

While many of the blogging services will provide a subdomain for free, you should invest in your own personal domain name. Not only will your blog appear more professional, but it will be easier for your readers to remember it.

Using a Pseudonym

There is another consideration when setting up and naming your blog—whether to use your own name. Should you use it to identify yourself to your readers or choose a pseudonym? There are pros and cons to using either.

The pros for using your own name are that if you are trying to establish yourself as a specialist in your chosen niche, you probably want to be recognized using your real name. And if your blog really takes off, the media may want to contact you for an arti-

CLICK TIP

If you are creating a pseudonym, make sure it's a memorable one by keeping it simple, short, and witty, if possible.

cle or quote. Wouldn't it be nice to see your name in print? The more popular your blog is, the better known you become.

The cons for using your own name are many. A pseudonym provides a cloak of anonymity that many users find comforting. A pen name is also helpful in providing a mask to conceal a writer's gender or that they are writing in more than one genre. A travel blogger may also want to disguise the fact that he is moonlighting from the boss. And if someone is writing controversial material, he will want to protect his reputation by using a different name.

If you decide to adopt a pen name make sure that it's available and another blogger isn't using the same one. That would be confusing for readers. Not only should you surf the internet for this information, but also check with the U.S. Copyright Office (copyright.gov).

CLICK TIP

Watching your blog's traffic closely will provide you with a good idea of your audience's reading habits, interests, and locations. You'll learn who is coming to see what, from where, and at what time.

Publishing Your Blog

Finding the most appropriate blog service or application can be an over-whelming process especially with the countless options available. This section will help you find a good blog platform that works best for you.

WARNING

Create a separate e-mail address for blogging purposes.

This will safeguard your personal or business e-mail address from spammers, stalkers, and any other potential security hazards that come with interacting with the public on the web.

There are two main types of blogging platforms—hosted service and server application. Both perform basically the same task of publishing a blog. Either will meet your needs, and each has been around long enough that the bugs have been worked out.

There are significant technological differences between hosted blogging services and installed server applications. The method you choose will have significant effects on how you run your blog.

Hosted Blogging Service

A hosted blogging service is entirely web-based like Gmail or PayPal. All of your interactions with the blogging service, including setting up and posting to your own blog, are done through the blogging service's website. There is nothing to download and nothing to install, and you can begin blogging immediately.

Blogging services have multiple levels of service, ranging from a basic free service to a more expensive, fully featured service. Fortunately, the top level of service isn't very expensive (approximately $15 to $30 a month).

One of the biggest disadvantages to hosted blogging services is the limited ability to customize your site. Some services allow more than others, but complete customization isn't possible as you won't have access to much of the code. However, most of these services have a lot of extra features that are easy to use and set up, and have a relatively low cost of entry. So if you're not handy with installing server software, this may be the best choice for you.

The following are some of the most popular web-based blogging services, although they are by no means the only quality services available:

→ *Blogger (blogger.com).* This is probably the most commonly used blogging service on the internet. It's great for first-time bloggers because its fast and easy to set up—and, it's free. Users are also not limited in terms of traffic, storage space, or even the number of blogs you can create.

→ *TypePad (typepad.com).* TypePad is another popular service, but it is not free. It has different levels of service, powerful features, attractive and easy-to-navigate blogs, extensive customization, and easy integration of revenue streams. Professional bloggers seem to prefer it because it does not cater to beginners.

→ *WordPress.com (wordpress.com).* Like Blogger, this is a free blogging service that is tailored to casual bloggers needing easy-to-use features. It is the web-based offspring of the downloadable WordPress.org application. Unlike Blogger, WordPress.com seems to have more restrictions, including the inability to have more than one blog. It also frowns on advertising networks or commercial blogging of any kind, making it a less than ideal choice for the professional blogger.

→ *Eponym (eponym.com).* Although fairly new to the blogosphere, this service is highly customizable and easy-to-use, plus it seems to be managed with professional bloggers in mind. There are six levels of service ranging from free to $39.95.

Installed Server Applications

Installed server applications are programs that you the user install on your own web server or web host account. Available blogging server applications range in size and quality, as well as in cost of operation.

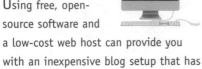

CLICK TIP

Using free, open-source software and a low-cost web host can provide you with an inexpensive blog setup that has plenty of room to grow in the future.

These types of application give you infinite control over your blog, which is great if you have familiarity with the code in which the application was written. And even if you don't, you'll probably find the application's base installation more than sufficient for your needs. In addition to registering a domain name, you will also have to pay hosting fees using this method, so you may find it a little more expensive in the beginning until the revenue starts coming in.

The major applications are:

➡ *Movable Type (sixapart.com/movabletype)*. This is a blogging application for the professional blogger that has a widely used platform with many features such as archiving, trackback, and visitor comments. This popular application has been around since 2001, and books, websites, reviews, and articles have been published to help users to master it. The Learning Movable Type website (learningmovabletype.com) is a good place to start.

➡ *LifeType (lifetype.com)*. This is a free, open-source blogging platform that has been designed to allow multiple blogs with multiple users in hopes of creating strong blog communities. Although it has many admirable qualities, it's not considered one of the best platforms for professional bloggers who just want to blog and not waste an hour looking through the menu for the right tools to use.

➡ *WordPress.org (wordpress.org)*. This application is the precursor to the WordPress.com web-based server. It's a free, open-source application, which means that you have access to all the code and can customize the whole application top to bottom. First-timers may find the installation process a bit daunting, although the administrative interface is easy to navigate once you are up and running.

Generating Traffic for Your Blog

The task of attracting tons of readers may seem somewhat daunting, but doing business on the internet has the wonderful advantage of automation.

This means directing traffic to your blog is a lot easier than you may think by utilizing some of the great services available. The main ways that readers will find your blog is through search engines, blog directories, link exchanges, and word of mouth.

Search Engines

As discussed in Chapter 6 for SEO, the number one way to promote your site is by letting the search engines know about it. Most of the top level engines will eventually find your site by using their web crawlers, but you want to give them a heads up so your site can be indexed more quickly for your viewing audience.

Keywords

I also discussed the importance of strategically using keywords on your website; these same guidelines apply to your blog. Find out which keywords and phrases are the most popular for your niche and plant them in your content. You can also implement an ad networking campaign like Google Adwords, mapped out in Chapter 7.

CLICK TIP

Keyword profitability is one factor used by professional bloggers when choosing a subject on which to base their blogs.

Blog Aggregators

A blog or news aggregator is a tool that retrieves RSS, Atom, or XML feeds from news sources, blogs, and other publishing platforms and pulls them altogether in one place. Wikipedia offers the best description for the function of an aggregator:

> Aggregators reduce the time and effort needed to regularly check websites for updates, creating a unique information space or "personal newspaper." Once subscribed to a feed, an aggregator is able to check for new content at user-determined intervals and retrieve the update. The content is sometimes described as being "pulled" to the subscriber, as opposed to "pushed" with e-mail or IM. Unlike recipients of some "pushed" information, the aggregator user can easily

unsubscribe from a feed." (Reprinted from en.wikipedia.org/wiki/ Aggregator under the GNU Free Documentation License.)

McDougall recommends enabling the RSS, Atom, or XML feed feature on your blogging platform and submitting it to all the aggregators you can find. For no extra work per post, you can make sure your blog is included in the search results of these popular tools. The following are some popular aggregator sites that you should submit your feed to:

- ➡ Technorati—technorati.com
- ➡ BlogExplosion—blogexplosion.com
- ➡ WebLogs—weblogs.com
- ➡ BlogRolling—blogrolling.com

Sue Freeman (newyorkoutdoors.wordpress.com) frequently makes use of blog aggregators to provide content for her blog. "Every day I get all of these different references to news or blog articles related to hiking, kayaking, and other outdoor activities," she says. "I pick up a lot of information through those feeds and if anything is relevant to New York State and outdoor recreation, I might write a short paragraph and link back to that particular blog or news article. So I'm kind of pointing people in the direction of where to find information."

CLICK TIP

Blog aggregators can lead new readers to your blog, but don't rely solely on them for new traffic. Your posts will be listed in among billions of other posts, so you'll have plenty of competition.

TrackBack

TrackBack is a communication mechanism specifically designed to get tons of links to your blog quickly scattered around the blogosphere to bring in flocks of readers. Exchanging TrackBack links is kind of like reciprocal linking—except better because you are connecting with other blogs to discuss the same topic. To participate, your blog must be equipped with TrackBack protocol; otherwise, it will not be able to read or send TrackBack links. If your blog platform does not support the protocol, search the internet for a supporting plug-in.

CLICK TIP

To generate more traffic to your site, submit your blog posts to blog carnivals. Find a list of relevant carnivals for your niche at Blog Carnival (blogcarnival.com/bc). Or enter keywords related to your niche and the words "blog carnival" into a search engine to find specific carnivals.

Link Exchanges

Swapping links with other bloggers is an excellent way to get your own blog noticed. Blog referrals from other bloggers have a high-percentage conversion rate because readers generally trust their favorite blogger's recommendations. As a refresher, go back and re-read the section on "Reciprocal Links" in Chapter 6 and remember to choose quality, relevant blogs to trade links with. Link exchanges are done in three main places: blogrolls, trackback, and post links.

Developing Links

James Hills (mantripping.com) says that HubPages (hubpages.com), Squidoo (squidoo.com), EzineArticles (ezinearticles.com), and WikiHow (wikihow.com) are great ways of developing links back to your site and improving your site's "authority" in the eyes of the search engines (as well as people).

Blogrolls

Blogrolls are simply a list of links that are usually displayed on a blog's sidebar. Kind of like a website's "favorite links" page. You can list whatever links you prefer, but hopefully they will be relevant to your own blog. You can also ask other blog owners to place your link on their blogrolls.

Freeman says that every once in a while she will get an e-mail from someone saying,

CLICK TIP

Surfing through blogrolls is a very common way for readers to find new blogs. Getting your blog listed in the blogrolls of other blogs will increase your traffic immediately.

BE OUR GUEST

According to James Hills, writing articles for other people's blogs (i.e., guest writer) is a fantastic way to build credibility because the blog owner is actually transferring his/her authority to you. "In effect, they are saying to their audience of 100, 1000, 100,000 people that you are worth listening to," he says. "And the search engines look at this too."

Hills goes on to say that guest writing gigs are sort of hit and miss, but once you become friendly with various bloggers, it's a cinch. "Pitching bloggers isn't much different than pitching an editor except they usually don't pay," he says. To start a relationship, e-mail the blog owner and suggest an article that you think would be great for his site—then offer to write it.

"I linked to your blog, will you link back?" And when looking at other blogs, she sometimes finds that her blog has been linked on the blogroll of other blogs. "So it's kind of this self-perpetuating network where bloggers interlink with each other," she says.

Word of Mouth

Promotion through word of mouth is one of the best forms of advertisement. Most blog platforms have an "e-mail this post to a friend" link that is a simple, yet effective tool. Once someone clicks that link to send the post to a

CLICK TIP

To generate interest in your blog, leave thoughtful, supportive, and/or helpful comments on other blogs. Just make sure it doesn't look like you're trolling for comments. After a few weeks, you should start to notice other people reciprocating.

friend, the e-snowball starts rolling and gaining momentum. McDougall reminds us that the real key to starting this word-of-mouth-traffic avalanche is creating unique and interesting, or extremely useful, content. "Nobody bothers to forward boring links to one another," he writes.

Profiting from Your Blog

The biggest incentive to creating, developing, and maintaining a popular blog is that it can be a reliable source of revenue. Naturally that's easier said than done, and some bloggers may be disappointed to find that there are no immediate "tangible" benefits from keeping a regular blog. "In the beginning there is not a lot of financial reward, so you need some other source of income until you get your audience going and get established," cautions Beth Whitman. While you shouldn't expect massive profits from starting ten blogs in a month's time, you can nonetheless find many financial benefits in keeping a frequently updated, well-written blog.

Throughout this book, and especially in Chapters 7, 8, and 10, I have discussed a variety of marketing opportunities. These include affiliate programs, paid listings, ad campaigns, article marketing, search engine marketing, and other strategies that can (and should) be used for generating revenue for your blog.

Another idea is a take-off on the subscription business model (Chapter 3) for paid memberships. The pay-for-access membership plan is fairly new to the blogosphere and has yet to be deemed a success or failure. The concept is simple: readers have to pay a subscription fee to read that particular blog. Or

---

WARNING

Keep in mind that unless you can find a plug-in that provides specific functions for your blogging platform or your service provides them, it will be necessary for you to do a little programming to implement them.

---

partial access may be granted for free to nonmembers, while paying members have free rein and enjoy all kinds of perks.

One more strategy that fits under the subscription business model umbrella is the "early edition" that allows subscribers to read posts a few hours (or even days) before the general public can. And finally, there is the "ad-free" version. It is probably the most successful membership blog strategy because anyone can still read the content. The only difference is that subscribers can read it without having to see your ads.

A subscription business model is not recommended for a blog just coming out of the starting gate because it limits traffic growth. Until your blog becomes a viable one that is drawing in a large readership, it's in your best interest to generate revenue through traditional means.

HOW TO USE AFFILIATE PROGRAMS ON YOUR BLOG

In Chapter 10, I'm going to talk in detail about using affiliate programs in conjunction with your travel site. But for blogging purposes, let's take a quick look at some of the questions you should ask yourself before using affiliate programs on your blog:

1. *Who are your readers?* Put yourself in your readers' shoes and think about what topics may appeal to them as they browse through your blog. Are there specific products or services they would be interested in? If so, how would you grab their attention?

2. *Do you know who you are linking to?* Look carefully at affiliate marketers' sites before providing a link to them. Sending blog readers to an unprofessional looking site featuring cheesy products will diminish your credibility.

3. *Can you personally endorse these products?* Before you recommend a product or service to your faithful readers, make sure you have some familiarity with it. Glowing reviews are always helpful, but honest opinions are even more valuable. For example, if you are promoting an itinerary watching service for mobile devices, a candid evaluation about why it might work better for some travelers than others will make you a trusted source and increase your readership.

AFFILIATE PROGRAMS ON YOUR BLOG, CONTINUED

4. *Are you embedding your contextual links?* Affiliate links embedded in your text typically have more clickability than a banner ad or text links placed along the side of your blog. To get readers' attention you need to plant the information right in front of them. For example, if you're writing about a specific travel destination such as archaeological sites in Greece, provide an Amazon affiliate link to a book about ancient Greece.

5. *How well are your affiliate links positioned?* Affiliate links need to be effectively positioned on your site to be noticed. If you are not going to embed the ads in a contextual link, place them on the side of the blog or at the bottom of a post for better visibility.

6. *Are you trying to hide something?* Internet browsers are pretty savvy and don't like it when bloggers think they can sneak affiliate links by them. You don't have to put a neon border around the links, but you shouldn't try to hide or camouflage them either. Just let readers know what kind of link they are clicking so they can make the choice to do so—or not.

7. *Are you tracking your visitors?* Most affiliate programs provide reports with visitor statistics so that you know what links are more effective than others. This gives you the opportunity to decide if link positions need to be alternated, if different keywords should be used, or if other marketing strategies should be implemented.

8. *Are you watching your traffic?* Obviously traffic levels are important when it comes to generating revenue from your blog. The more people who visit, the more people will read your blog and see your affiliate links. Implement some of the search engine marketing strategies discussed in this chapter to increase your traffic levels.

9. *How broad are your horizons?* There are tons of travel products and services to promote, so don't limit yourself to just one or two affiliate marketers. At the same time, be careful about endorsing too many products and cluttering up your site. This could have a watered-down effect and turn off your readers.

10. *Are you implementing other revenue streams?* Don't limit yourself to just one advertising program. Affiliate links work well with other revenue streams, including AdSense campaigns. Use and combine several different advertising programs to increase profits generated by your site. Just be careful not to clutter your site with too many programs that detract from your site's content—and main purpose.

Beth Whitman's blog, Wanderlust and Lipstick (wanderlustandlipstick), is a great example of a multiple-user blog featuring a community forum, travel tips, information, stories, photo gallery, product sales, newsletter signup, and more. See Figure 9.1.

Figure 9.1: **WANDERLUST AND LIPSTICK BLOG**

Chapter 10

The Travel Affiliate

"*T*ime is money" is an old cliché everyone knows and understands, especially here in the United States. According to recent research sponsored by Expedia, Americans have an average of 12 vacation days a year (far fewer than workers in many other nations) but still find themselves unable to use them all. Researchers found that one-third of workers fail to use all their vacation days—leaving a whopping 421 million "days off" on the table each year. Industry experts say these statistics reflect

Americans' growing "time poverty"—the need to do more and more in less and less time. Time poverty is the number-one trend driver in the travel industry, they say.

So what does this mean for you? For starters, Tom Ogg, author of the *Home Based Travel Affiliate* (Tom Ogg & Associates, 2007), says the travel and tourism industry is dominating the internet with more than 50 percent of all travel transactions taking place online. "Airlines, hotels, car rental companies, resorts, cruises, tours, sightseeing attractions, and other travel oriented services are increasing their web marketing and looking to maximize their online transactions as being the most profitable and efficient way to do business," he writes. "Travel and tourism is spending hundreds of millions of dollars to market its wares on the web . . . now you can cash in big time."

One of the fastest ways to capitalize on this rapidly growing trend is to start generating revenue from your website or blog through an affiliate program. This is one of the internet's most effective marketing tools, and there are hundreds of merchants waiting in the wings to put cash in your pocket. Just think: before the end of the day you could ring up your first sale! But before you get too excited, first you need to understand affiliate marketing so that you can make it work for you.

What Is Affiliate Marketing?

Affiliate marketing can essentially be defined as a method of online selling by proxy. This means an affiliate marketer does not need to have her own service or product to sell. Instead, she can join a program allowing her to promote another merchant's product and receive a commission for any sales or leads that are generated. (Note: Wherever affiliate "products" are referred to throughout this chapter, the same usually applies for affiliate "services.")

Cost Per Sale

The most common affiliate model is when an affiliate marketer advertises a product on their website and links to the site of the affiliate merchant via ads, banners, or text links. When a visitor to the affiliate site follows the link and purchases the product, the affiliate marketer receives a prearranged percentage.

Many programs are designed so the affiliate marketer receives a commission on anything the customer spends on the merchant's site, even if he doesn't purchase the originally advertised product. However, a few affiliate programs mandate the customer has to buy the actual product the affiliate marketer is promoting to receive a commission.

Cost Per Lead (or Action)

Other affiliate programs are service or sign-up based, rather than product based. Instead of buying a product when they reach the merchant's site, customers are only required to sign up to a list, newsletter, or other service, for the affiliate to receive his payment.

Cost Per Click

This is a very popular affiliate revenue model sponsored by ad networks such as Google AdSense (google.com/adsense) and Yahoo! Publisher Network (publisher .yahoo.com). These programs place content related ads on the affiliate's web page. For affiliates to receive a commission visitors need only to click the link—no other type of transaction is required.

CLICK TIP

Contextual advertising through affiliate marketing has made it possible for millions of website owners to profitably engage in e-commerce in small but highly effective means.

How Affiliate Marketing Works

The concept of affiliate marketing is actually pretty straightforward; however, it gets buried underneath piles of terminology and lingo so that its simplicity is often overlooked. In a nutshell: affiliate marketing is earning a commission or fee by selling products or services for someone else. Although it sounds easy enough, some common questions about affiliate marketing are:

➡ How will the merchant know the customer was referred from my site?
➡ Will I only get paid for purchases or will I get paid for every lead?
➡ What does revenue share mean?

This section answers these questions by explaining the basic process and some of the models behind affiliate marketing.

Affiliate Tracking

Affiliate marketing is built on the ability to track web visitors so affiliates can get paid for their referrals. This program tracking method is generally very effective and uses a combination of techniques to ensure affiliates get the rewards they are entitled to. These systems include affiliate codes, tracking URL, cookie tracking, and IP tracking.

Affiliate or Referral Codes

When you join an affiliate program, you will be issued an affiliate account with a unique affiliate code, also known as a referral code. Visitors to your site will be supplied with this affiliate code to use when they buy a product from the affiliate merchant, and it will link them to you ensuring you get your commission.

But what happens if your visitors forget to enter your referral code when they buy an affiliate product? This is entirely possible, which is why affiliate codes are only one of the tracking processes used in combination with several others.

Tracking URL

The goal is to have your customers visit the merchant site via a text link, ad, or banner placed on your site. When this happens, your affiliate code automatically forms a part of the linking URL used and is picked up by the merchant site so that it can credit you with the referral. However, if a visitor leaves your site and later returns to the merchant's site directly to make a purchase, you would not be credited for the referral unless cookie tracking was implemented.

Cookie Tracking

If a potential customer visits an affiliate merchant through your site's link, a cookie containing your affiliate code is transferred to its computer. If the visitor buys something from the affiliate merchant, the information from the cookie is read and the sales lead is credited to your affiliate account.

Some cookies expire as soon as the visitor navigates away from the merchant site, while others remain valid eternally. Typically, cookies will remain valid between 30 and 90 days. Finding an affiliate program with longer cookie validity will increase your potential for affiliate commissions.

> ## Words of Wisdom
>
> *The way to get started is to quit talking and begin doing.*
>
> —WALT DISNEY

IP Tracking

It's no secret that many web users regularly clear their computers of cookies or use software that blocks cookies from being stored because they have privacy concerns. For this reason, it makes sense to combine cookie tracking with IP tracking to make it as effective as possible.

Here's how it works: When a customer arrives at the affiliate merchant's site via a link from your site, the merchant will recognize the affiliate code in the tracking URL. It will also register the IP address of the customer's computer, linking it with the affiliate code. So, when future purchases are made from that IP address, the sales lead will be credited to you even if there is no cookie on the computer containing your affiliate code.

> ## Words of Wisdom
>
> *Having all the content in the world loaded with affiliate links is just an effort in futility if no one comes to read the content and click on the links. There are many strategies for driving traffic to travel oriented websites, and much depends on the value proposition that your site offers.*
>
> —TOM OGG, AUTHOR OF
> *HOME BASED TRAVEL AFFILIATE*

How Effective Is Affiliate Tracking?

There will always be a few customers who fall through the affiliate net. Perhaps a customer sees a great work-related product advertised on your site while he is surfing the net on his home computer. However, he might wait until consulting with his manager and buy it directly from the merchant site using his office computer. Unfortunately, you will miss out on the referral because he will not have an identifying cookie on his office computer, and the merchant will not associate his IP address with you.

These situations are the exception, not the rule. They should not detract from the power of affiliate marketing. With the increased use of laptops in the workplace, people tend to use the same computer most of the time. It is estimated that affiliate tracking is currently 99 percent effective, and as more complex forms of tracking are introduced, things can only get better.

Affiliate Payment Models

As previously discussed, the basic principle behind most affiliate programs is that a customer follows a link, banner, or ad from your site to a merchant's site. If a purchase is made, you get paid a commission. However, there are different payment models you may come across when looking for affiliate programs. It helps to have an understanding of the various terms and abbreviations related to affiliate payments.

Some of payment terms you might come across are:

1. *PPA—Pay Per Action/Pay Per Acquisition; PPS—Pay Per Sale; PPO—Pay Per Order.* These abbreviations refer to the most popular payment model for affiliate programs. It means that no payment is generated until a referred visitor makes a predefined action on the merchant site, which is usually buying something. This model is generally favored by merchants because they only have to pay a commission when something is sold.

2. *PPL—Pay Per Lead.* With this model you receive a payment for every qualified lead you send to the merchant's site. The definition of a qualified lead will vary by program, but it usually means your visitor completes a particular act on the merchant's site such as filling in a form or providing an e-mail address.

3. *PPC—Pay Per Click.* This model generates a payment as soon as a visitor to your site clicks on a link to the merchant's site, even if they don't buy anything. The nature of this model means the payments for each click are likely to be relatively low, so you will need to drive a lot of traffic to the merchant's site to make it worthwhile.

4. *PPM—Pay Per Impression.* With this model, a payment is generated as soon as a visitor to your site views a web page showing a particular ad,

regardless if whether she clicks the link or not. It is rare to find this payment model in relation to an affiliate program, and you will be required to guarantee a high level of traffic to your site to qualify.

CLICK TIP

A recent survey conducted by E-consultancy.com revealed that affiliate marketing is the most cost-effective means for driving customer acquisition, with travel companies making the best use of this channel.

5. *Revenue share or lifetime value.* Here you may not receive anything for the initial lead, but you will get a share of anything that customer spends in the future. The duration of revenue share programs varies from a month to several years; there are even lifetime value programs enabling you to continue receiving commissions on any of your customers' purchases indefinitely. The individual payments in these programs tend to be lower, but the payout is better in the long run if your customer makes regular purchases.

Advantages of Affiliate Marketing

Affiliate marketing has a number of advantages over selling products of your own. They include:

➡ *Low overhead.* You don't have product production, order processing, storage, shipping, or customer service issues to worry about.

➡ *Low risk.* Someone else has invested the money in researching and developing the product. Start with affiliate networks, and as you become acclimated in the world of affiliate marketing, you can branch out and look for trustworthy affiliate merchants.

➡ *Low startup costs.* All you really need is a website, blog, or online newsletter to get started. The affiliate merchant should provide everything else you need in terms of marketing materials.

How to Use Affiliate Programs

Most affiliate marketers choose to promote affiliate products through their website. They may either have a separate site or page for each product, or advertise several related products together. Affiliate links can be embedded into your site using text links, ads, banners, or a full sales page. In addition to a web page, there are a number of other potential channels for promoting your affiliate programs. There are a number of ideas to get started.

➡ *Include affiliate links in viral e-books.* A viral e-book is one that spreads quickly throughout the online community, being passed from one person to the next, creating maximum exposure. You might not make much money from the initial sale of the e-book, but you can make a steady income from affiliate links incorporated into it. To make an e-book viral you need to have high-quality, well-written content and sell the book for a reasonable price—or give it away free. Then give buyers the resale rights so that they can choose to sell or give it away. As the distribution of the e-book widens, so does the promotion of your business and affiliate links.

➡ *Write articles relating to your affiliate products.* Producing a relevant article that contains an affiliate link to the merchant site is a very simple way to generate affiliate income. The article can be submitted to several article directories and e-zines, creating a great deal of exposure for your affiliate link. Most directories won't allow a full-scale sales pitch about your affiliate product, but a general article, perhaps addressing a problem that your affiliate product or services might solve, would be appropriate. Chapter 7 discusses the benefits of article marketing in more detail.

➡ *Give away a free report related to your affiliate products.* People appreciate valuable information, and they love freebies. So sending out free

CLICK TIP

Too busy to write your own e-book? Rebrandable e-books are available on the internet for immediate download. They can be easily customized with your business information and affiliate links. Search for "rebrandable e-books" on any search engine to see what is available in your specialty.

reports is always well-received. One of the most effective ways to do this is to produce a report in multiple parts—one to be e-mailed every day for a week or once a week for a month. This gives you repeated opportunities to soft-sell your product or service to your customers. You could also focus each report on a different affiliate product.

➡ *Write blog posts or comments including your affiliate link.* If you have your own blog (and you should), it can be a great forum to promote affiliate products. Regular visitors will respect your opinion and are more likely to buy a product recommended by you than one simply advertised on a merchant site. Be subtle in your sales pitch and mention a product a few times before providing an affiliate link to it.

You can also visit other relevant blogs and comment on posts relating to your affiliate products. Writing a valuable and insightful comment that really addresses the issues in the blog post will encourage people to follow your affiliate link and buy products that you endorse. You can read more about the power of blogging in Chapter 9.

Getting Started in Affiliate Marketing

Once your website is established, setting yourself up as an affiliate marketer is relatively simple. The basic steps include finding your niche (discussed in Chapter 2), gauging the demand in your field or expertise, and selecting appropriate affiliate programs.

FIVE THINGS TO LOOK FOR IN AN AFFILIATE PROGRAM

1. *A high quality product.* Every time you personally recommend or promote a product you are putting your reputation and credibility on the line. For this reason you want to be certain the affiliate products you choose are of the highest quality. Promoting an inferior product will greatly reduce your chances of building up

FIVE THINGS TO LOOK FOR IN AN
AFFILIATE PROGRAM, CONTINUED

a profitable affiliate business in the long run. Testing the product yourself can reassure you that it is of sufficient quality and will also help you put together a genuine and believable sales pitch.

2. *A product that is relevant to your niche*. Finding products that are closely related to the content of your website means that you have a well-targeted audience to sell to. Have a good knowledge of the visitors to your site and what they are searching for. This will help you choose suitable affiliate products. Finding products that fulfill the needs of your visitors is the key to successful affiliate marketing.

3. *Merchant stability*. Look for established merchants who are financially stable with a reputation for reliability. Using an established affiliate network when first starting out can help you to minimize risk and ensure you get commissions you're entitled to.

4. *A supportive merchant*. You should always be able to contact your affiliate merchants, even when using affiliate managers. If they are easy to reach, helpful in resolving any issues, and proactive in helping you to increase your sales potential, the affiliate programs are likely to be a success.

As well as up-to-date banners, ads, and promotional materials, your merchants should provide you with a reporting method to enable you to see how many visitors you are referring and how much commission you are generating. Real time, online reporting is the best option, but any sort of reporting will enable you to target your marketing more effectively.

5. *A great sales page for the product*. The sales or landing page is the part of the merchant's website that customers are directed to when they click on your affiliate link, ad, or banner. It's the first impression they get of the product you are recommending, so it is crucial that it meets their expectations. A badly constructed sales page will discredit the merchant as well as the person who referred them (i.e., you). So check out the sales page thoroughly. If it's appealing, easy to navigate, and professional looking, then you are likely to get a good conversion rate.

Your Travel Niche

First you will want to look for affiliate products that relate to your current travel niche. Then you can incorporate affiliate ads, banners, and text links into existing web pages, or add a dedicated sales page promoting your affiliate product.

Travel Product Demand

Before you launch an affiliate marketing campaign for your travel business it's always a good idea to be sure there is enough demand for that type of product in the targeted travel niche. Here are some ways you can determine levels of demand for your niche:

➡ *Keyword research.* Keyword research is one of the best ways to discover what browsers are looking for in relation to your niche. As discussed in Chapter 6, there are a number of keyword tools that can generate common keyword phrases relating to your niche and tell you how often they are entered into the search engines. Two common tools are Keyword Discovery (keyworddiscovery.com) and WordTracker (freekeywords.wordtracker.com).

➡ *Affiliate program research.* Confirm there are enough affiliate programs operating within your specialty to allow you to be selective about those you join. Next, check out the programs to see what the payment models and levels of commission are. Some programs have lower payments or more stringent guidelines than others, and you want to get a reasonable return without a lot of headaches.

➡ *Look at your competitors.* Don't be intimidated by a little competition. If there seem to be a large number of affiliate marketers operating in your chosen niche, it generally means there is a lot of demand. But as long as you have quality affiliate products to promote, you should still do well. However, if there are hundreds of marketers with limited affiliate programs to choose from, you may have trouble making your site different enough to attract new customers.

➡ *Ask questions in discussion forums.* Online social networking, including blogs, discussion forums, and membership sites, have really taken off in the last few years. Joining relevant sites and finding out what people

CLICK TIP

Broaden your horizons by including international travelers in your marketing campaign. The Travel Industry Association recently reported that travel spending for both domestic and international travelers is expected to reach more than $778 billion by the end of 2008.

are talking about, as well as the kind of products they are looking for, can help you focus on your specialty. Plus building a good online reputation with other members on these sites is beneficial for networking.

Join Affiliate Programs

Now comes the fun part—taking the plunge! There are two types of affiliate programs; those managed though an affiliate network and those managed by individual merchants. Both have advantages and disadvantages.

Some merchants prefer to have their affiliate programs managed through affiliate networks such as Commission Junction (cj.com), Linkshare (linkshare.com), and The Pepperjam Network (pepperjamnetwork.com). Setting up an account with one of these networks is quick, easy, and free. It's also a good opportunity for an affiliate marketer just starting out because there are hundreds of affiliate programs to choose from with very little risk involved. The downside can be that the commission payments tend to be lower than merchant managed programs as the network takes a fee for each sale before your commission is calculated.

CLICK TIP

Ruthlessly compare your site to competitors' sites and ask yourself what they are doing better? Make a detailed list and then go back to your site and implement those changes.

Independent affiliate programs are not hard to find with a little research. Simply typing a couple of keywords along with the word "affiliate" into a search engine should generate some desirable results. Entering the words "travel" and "affiliate" yields hundreds of results, so narrow your search by including travel interests. By adding the word "cooking," a new search page returned some very interesting results including cooking DVDs for destinations like India and Greece.

If you have a particular merchant in mind, visit that site to see if it has an affiliate program. Merchant managed programs generally pay better commissions but there are sometimes more risks involved, especially since you are relying on the merchant to pay you directly.

FIVE COMMON AFFILIATE MARKETING MISTAKES TO AVOID

1. *Not knowing your website traffic.* To find an affiliate program that is really targeted to your particular audience, you have to know your customers. How old are they? Are they frequent business travelers? Do they want luxury accommodations? Or are they budget conscious? What do they like to do for relaxation? Why did they visit your site? If you don't know your customers, it will be difficult finding suitable affiliate products for them.

2. *Failing to pre-sell the product.* Unless you are using AdSense (more on that later) it's not enough to get your customers to follow an ad or link to the merchant site; they have to be ready to buy or sign up for something when they get there. And if your customer was not expecting to be redirected to another site, chances are they will either hit the back button or click away, leaving everyone in the dust. What this means is a well-designed affiliate site should have sold the product before the customer arrives at the merchant site.

3. *Joining too many affiliate programs.* Because affiliate programs are easy to sign up for, you can end up promoting a huge number of products without time to devote to each individual one. Carefully select a handful of products to begin with. Starting with just a few can give you the experience you need as well as the opportunity to experiment with different affiliate marketing techniques. Once you have found a method that works you can begin to expand your portfolio. Also, be consistent with the products you are promoting and only choose one from each category. For example, if you endorse more than one itinerary-watching service or several travel insurance companies, visitors will be confused about which one is best.

FIVE COMMON AFFILIATE MARKETING MISTAKES TO AVOID, CONTINUED

4. *Focusing on advertising rather than content.* A common myth is if you have a lot of useful and informative content, your visitors will not click ads or links because they will not want to leave your site. Not true. The reality is if you have great content on your site, you will gain credibility with your visitors. This means they will be more comfortable about buying a product you recommended. To make an affiliate income you need to attract targeted traffic to your website. Providing excellent content is one the best ways to achieve that.

5. *Having an impersonal site.* You will have more success convincing visitors to buy a particular product if you have injected some of your personality into your site. Personal endorsements of a product are generally more effective than a banner or standard ad, so write your own product reviews with a personal a touch. Including information about yourself on your site, such as a photo and personal interests, helps visitors feel more connected to you, which instills a degree of trust.

Starting Your Own Affiliate Program

So far this chapter has focused on selling someone else's product as an affiliate marketer; but what if you have your own product to sell and are looking to set up your own affiliate program? An affiliate program is a great way to promote brand awareness, so here are a few things to think about before getting started:

The advantages of having your own affiliate program:

➡ Running an affiliate program is similar to having a large sales team promoting your product and only paying them when they actually sell something.

➡ Advertising and endorsements for your product or company appear on numerous sites, bringing awareness and exposure of your brand to a larger audience.

➡ An affiliate program significantly increases targeted traffic to your site. Although it is still up to you to make the sale once your visitors arrive, your overall sales and profits should increase considerably.

> **CLICK TIP**
>
> Find more information on affiliate programs at associateprograms.com or refer-it.com.

Methods of Starting an Affiliate Program

There are three options to consider when starting your own affiliate product: joining an affiliate network, using web-based software, and build it yourself. Each has its strengths.

Joining an affiliate network is the simplest method because it requires the least amount of work upfront. Working with an established network is easy, and it will have ready-made reporting tools available. Plus networks find and manage your affiliates for you. The downside of using affiliate networks is that the ongoing costs can be quite high because you usually have to pay a fee for each sale in addition to the initial sign-up costs.

A less expensive solution is to use web-based affiliate software. As with the network, this option allows you to sell products from your site and have affiliates sign up to promote your products. However, the management of the program is performed by the software. Wed-based affiliate software packages should provide you with a shopping cart and reporting functions to provide details of your affiliate partners, as well as facilities to e-mail receipts and offer a variety of shipping options.

Building and managing your own affiliate program involves the greatest outlay of time and possibly money initially, but it may be the most cost-effective solution in the long run. You need to host the program yourself and manage product campaigns, affiliate data, sales information, and commission payments. If you have a large number of products

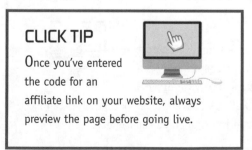

> **CLICK TIP**
>
> Once you've entered the code for an affiliate link on your website, always preview the page before going live.

to promote, it is worth investing in building your own affiliate program, especially if your products are of a high value.

Dan Parlow, CEO and co-founder of MyTripJournal.com, created brand awareness for his site through affiliate marketing and custom branding. The founders started by branding their site for Lonely Planet (lonelyplanet.com), one of the largest online travel guidebooks in the world. This eventually led to custom branding for 15 different partners. "The biggest surprise we had as we developed My Trip Journal was the number of people in RVs who had laptops," says Parlow. "So we formed a relationship with the Good Sam Club (goodsamclub.com), who are the largest RV club in the world, and then a bunch of related websites owned by the same group of companies. The RV traffic is about 50 percent of our total traffic now." See Figure 10.1.

Making Sense of Google AdSense

Google AdSense is a popular method of PPC advertising that allows other website owners to publish Google text and image advertisements on your website. Based on criteria you select, Google displays ads related to your site's content, and each time a visitors clicks one, you receive a commission. How much revenue is generated really depends on the amount of traffic to your site.

Two new developments by Google AdSense involve video keyword advertising as well as pay-per-thousand-impressions. Currently, Google is looking into the idea of using a cost-per-action based service, which would only involve paying the search service if someone actually takes "action" toward making a purchase.

CLICK TIP

George Simpson (georgesimpson.com), an expert in advertising, marketing, and internet trade media relations, recommends that travel entrepreneurs consider aggregating their sites with other related sites in the industry, like Travel Ad Network (traveladnetwork.com). This can be an alternative to using AdSense or in addition to using an ad campaign.

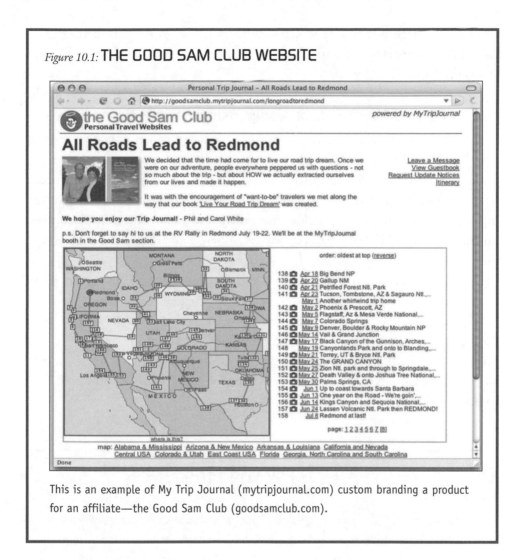

Figure 10.1: **THE GOOD SAM CLUB WEBSITE**

This is an example of My Trip Journal (mytripjournal.com) custom branding a product for an affiliate—the Good Sam Club (goodsamclub.com).

What are the advantages of using Google AdSense? Many users prefer this system to banner advertising because the ads are unobtrusive and relevant to the site's content. AdSense is also an easy system to use—even for beginners. Members simply install a script code onto the desired web page and a list of advertisements will appear where designated. Many web owners have found that AdSense can be very effective with helping online businesses generate additional advertising revenue. These are small businesses that would otherwise not have the capacity to create complex marketing campaigns and hire sales personnel. However, you must work hard to profit substantially from this service.

Tips on How to Make Money Using Google AdSense

Part of your strategy will be finding innovative ways to bring traffic to your site. This may include online advertising, but is certainly not limited to it. Some web owners have found that advertising their website in other media has successfully generated traffic. Like any other venue of internet advertising, website owners must provide interesting and keyword relevant content on their website. This will attract the best AdSense ads that pay out the most money whenever they are clicked.

While users are encouraged to use copy on their site that suggests users click on the ads, they are not allowed to directly use deliberate phrases such as "click on my ads." For a good example of how AdSense works, visit Blogspot.com. There you will notice popular blogs include a block of ads accompanied by the phrase "Sponsored Links" or "Advertisements." Working with a blogging service like this makes your job easy because you don't have to personally install any code on your website.

HANDY KEYWORD TOOL

To make money with AdSense, you have to think of your project as a marketing campaign, which means your travel niche market needs to be easily found using targeted keywords. One of the ways you can do this is by doing keyword research online. Fortunately, Google can also help you with this. Just go to AdWords.google.com/select/KeywordToolExternal. This keyword tool allows you to research popular or obscure keywords and find out what phrases are synonymous with them. These are identical keywords that users search for along with your chosen keyword. You can also search according to category or even price range. (For example, try searching for words with an average CPC/Cost Per Click of $20.)

Here to Stay

Affiliate marketing is a real buzzword among internet marketers, and it is set to remain a popular form of online selling for many years to come. With so many online businesses looking to promote their products and services, there is a great deal of profit to be made as an affiliate marketer.

However, the amount of work involved in successful affiliate marketing should not be underestimated. Some people believe that once you sign up as an affiliate you can just sit back and let the profits roll in. Sadly, this is not the case. Creating a successful travel affiliate marketing business takes just as much effort as any other business. Fully researching your niche and targeted market, updating your website, keeping current with the latest online selling techniques, and ensuring that you are providing excellent service and high quality products to your customers all take a certain amount of time and commitment. But if you are prepared to put in the necessary effort, affiliate marketing could be your rags-to-riches story.

Travel Affiliate Programs

There are hundreds of travel affiliate opportunities that you can take advantage of. They are too numerous to list in this book. However, we are going to provide you with a sample of available programs in the Appendix—Internet Resource Guide. Some of these programs are operated through affiliate networks, while others are independently managed by merchants.

When considering an affiliate program, carefully review the terms and conditions and be certain your site falls within the parameters of the guidelines. And remember: NO spamming! Using spam e-mail as a marketing strategy is a huge no-no and will quickly get you blacklisted from the affiliate merchant's program.

Chapter 11

Secure
Solutions

*P*utting together a website does not guarantee that you are on the road to riches. And, unfortunately, that road is going to be uneven and bumpy along the way. Whether you are a newcomer to the industry or have been in the trenches for a while, there are security concerns you need to be aware of.

Risky Business

Because online security is such a big issue, you will need to take safety measures to protect yourself and your computer. The risks of not adequately securing your business network and PCs are huge. Remember, not only is your data at risk from hacker attacks initiated through viruses, spyware, and other devious means, but your customers' personal and financial information is also in jeopardy. Peter Alexander cites the following facts from *Consumer Reports* in his Entrepreneur.com article, "Crafting a Technology Security Plan":

➡ During a recent 24-hour monitoring period, computer security software firm Symantec recorded 59 million attempts by hackers to gain unauthorized entry into business and home computers.

➡ In a survey, one out of four computer users said they had experienced a major, costly problem due to a computer virus. The average cost per incident was $109. In addition, one out of every 115 people was the victim of a scam e-mail attack, which cost victims an average of $850.

➡ To combat viruses and spyware, American consumers spent at least $7.8 billion for computer repairs, parts, and replacement over the past two years.

Business owners must constantly be vigilant because new security threats evolve and persistently hack away at their backdoors. Protect customers' data by encrypting it, thereby making it unreadable. Many types of financial and database software have encryption programs built into them. In the event yours doesn't, you can purchase and install an encryption program that is only accessible by a password or key.

WARNING

If a password is a word that can be found in the dictionary, it may be susceptible to "dictionary" attacks, which is when hackers attempt to guess passwords based on words in the dictionary.

Alexander also recommends that business owners take the following safety measures to secure their networks:

→ *Antivirus protection.* Spyware has become increasingly malicious, difficult to detect, and difficult to remove. An antispyware program that frequently downloads updated definitions and monitors activity in the background is important given the insidious nature of spyware.

→ *Firewall.* A firewall is designed to block unauthorized access to computers and networks. Firewalls are available in hardware (as standalone network security devices or integrated into network routers) or as software. A software firewall is particularly important for laptop users who travel. Firewall software is usually included in internet security suites, which also offer antivirus, antispyware, and other tools. Some software firewalls are even available in free, basic versions.

→ *Virtual private network (VPN).* A VPN creates a secure "tunnel" between a computer and an unsecured, public network, such as the internet. VPN technology offers an important layer of protection for your business's weakest security link—mobile user. VPN security can be integrated into some network devices, such as intelligent routers, and turned on or off as needed.

→ *Wireless security.* If your business uses a wireless network, at a minimum you should use a password, WEP key, or some other method to block unauthorized users from gaining access.

→ *Secure network hardware.* Ideally, your company's network should be protected by routers with comprehensive, built-in security, including integrated firewall, VPN, and an intrusion prevention system.

→ *Data protection.* Implementing regular backup procedures is a simple way to safeguard critical business and customer data. Setting permissions and encryption will also help.

Implementing a solid security plan is a big undertaking. If it seems overwhelming, outsource the job to an IT person or network security firm. Whatever you do, do it today.

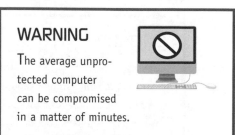

WARNING

The average unprotected computer can be compromised in a matter of minutes.

Have a Backup Plan

It's a fact: more than 300 million PCs and laptops are not backed up on a regular basis, leaving businesses vulnerable and primed for loss of precious data in the event of a computer crash. Usually there is no warning about an imminent crash, which can be caused by any number of things. A nasty virus or worm could be nestled deep inside, or it could be something as simple as a failed attempt to install a new software program. Often the reasons are completely unknown. In any event if your data is not backed up, the consequences could be devastating.

Here are some options to consider for developing a backup plan:

→ *Recordable media.* Once upon a time folks backed up their computers on a dozen or so floppy discs or to a zip drive. But now we have the convenience of rewritable drives that can record data on CDs and DVDs. Just make sure your computer's burn software has the ability to compress files, otherwise you may still end up with multiple discs.

→ *Second hard drive.* Another option is to install a second hard drive that mirrors the first hard drive. Internal hard drives are relatively easy to install, but can be subject to the same security risks as the primary hard drive. An external, removable hard drive may be a better alternative, although it will cost almost twice as much.

→ *Online backup service.* This type of service enables you to upload data and backup files to remote services via the internet. The restoration procedure is quick and easy, simply log onto the backup service and start the download process. Of course, this might be a problem if you don't have internet access because your computer crashed. Bottom

---

CLICK TIP

Laptops are a prime target for theft when traveling. To reduce the risk of yours being stolen, keep it inconspicuous by keeping it out of sight in a backpack or tote bag, instead of a tell-tale laptop case. Also, keep bags containing laptops closed, preferably locked.

line: this is a simple and inexpensive solution, but have an alternate backup plan in case this one fails.

➡ *Automatic backup software*. Make things easy and install software on your computer that will run in the background and back up whatever you are working on every few minutes, whether it's offsite or using the same rewritable CD over and over. Reliable services are Symantec's GoBack (symantec.com) and Genie Backup Manager (genie-soft.com).

➡ *Drive imaging*. This innovative, new software actually mirrors everything on your computer. In the event your hard drive fails or is corrupted beyond repair, you can restore all of your data and applications within minutes. This means you don't have to spend a couple of hours reinstalling all of the programs that were on the old hard drive. Traditional backup software will back up whatever files you designate, including photos, music, spreadsheets, and documents. But drive imaging programs act like a clone by duplicating everything on your computer to be transferred to another hard drive. For more information, take a look at Symantec's Norton Ghost 12.0 (symantec.com) or Acronis True Image 11 Home (acronis.com).

Credit Card Fraud

Crooks love the World Wide Web because they can hide behind a veil of virtual anonymity while carrying out their dirty little deeds. One of the biggest problems online is identity theft, where hackers compromise computer databases and steal customers' credit card information. In this chapter we've provided suggestions on how to protect your database from savvy internet hackers; however, another issue is the misuse of stolen credit card numbers, which can cause big losses for your travel business if not caught in time.

For card-present, in-store transactions, liability for fraud belongs to the credit card issuer. For card-not-present transactions, including online transactions, liability for fraud shifts to the online business owner. That means you will not receive payment for fraudulent online transactions. Don't let this stop you from doing business online, but take steps to limit your risk.

One of your most important fraud prevention steps is to deal with established, reputable merchant account providers (the acquiring bank) and processors. Your payment gateway provider (where authorizations and payments are processed) should offer real-time credit card authorization results to prevent charges on cards that have been reported as lost or stolen, or that are no longer valid for any other reason.

Use an address verification service that matches the cardholder billing address on file with the billing address submitted. Use card security codes,

DIGITAL CERTIFICATES

A digital certificate is a secure socket layer server certificate (aka SSL certificate) that protects and encrypts personal and financial information customers send to you over the internet. This is a must-have for any online business owner who wants to safely and securely process credit card orders.

Most web hosts like GoDaddy.com and Netfirms.com provide SSL certificates as part of their hosting package (or separately, if desired). You can also buy the service directly from these reliable providers:

- ➡ VeriSign—verisign.com
- ➡ GeoTrust—geotrust.com
- ➡ Trustwave—trustwave.com
- ➡ Thawte—thawte.com
- ➡ Network Solutions—networksolutions.com

Customers need to know they can trust you to protect their sensitive information, and they will feel more confident about doing business with you when you display the seal of an SSL certificate on your website. This lets them know your business has been authenticated and your site is secure.

For an added layer of protection, the Merchant Risk Council (MRC) recommends that business owners incorporate an Extended Validation SSL certificate, or EV SSL. This requires a stricter issuance process that goes to greater lengths to stamp out internet fraud. For more information, visit its website at merchantriskcouncil.org.

which are numbers that appear on Visa, MasterCard, and American Express cards that are never printed on receipts. The ability of a customer to provide these codes is additional assurance that the actual card is in the possession of the person conducting the transaction.

CLICK TIP

Develop a negative card and shipping address list and cross-check orders against it. Many criminals return to the same merchant to make fraudulent transactions.

Scambusters (scambusters.org) offers more preventive steps in its article entitled, "Eight Sure-Fire Strategies Any Business Owner Can Use to Reduce Credit Card Fraud." One tip is to be cautious about taking orders from people using free e-mail services. Before processing the order, send an email asking for additional information such as the exact name and billing address for the card, and the verification number. If you receive a response (don't be surprised if you don't), simply verify the information with the issuing bank. If you don't receive a response, the only loss is your time. Also, don't hesitate to pick up the phone and call the customer to confirm the order, which is another way to find out if this is a legitimate cardholder.

Chapter 12

Financial and Business Management

*T*he best indicator of how serious you are about your online travel business is how you handle the money. And if you're serious about your business, you need to be serious about the money. Basically there are two sides to the issue of money: how much you need to start and operate, and how much you can expect to take in. Doing this type of research is often difficult for entrepreneurs who would rather escort a tour group around Chinatown or redesign a new travel affiliate site than be bound to a desk dealing with tiresome numbers. But to be successful, you're going to have to force yourself to do it anyway.

Startup Funds

Many online travel business owners start out part-time and eventually segue into a full-time business as time and money permit. This gives entrepreneurs the opportunity to generate sufficient income to cover expenses and make a profit without borrowing a big chunk of change—at least initially. Although you can easily spend thousands of dollars starting a new business, you can just as easily get by with the bare essentials when starting an online business.

Because most online business owners get started with equipment and inventory they already own, it takes very little cash to get started with an e-commerce business. But if you want to create a real business, you need to be prepared to deal with startup economics and financial management.

How much money you need in the beginning depends on a number of factors such as whether you will have to upgrade your computer and get new

---

DO YOU HAVE A LICENSE FOR THAT?

The good news about an online travel business is that there are not any tests to pass or homework to do to become a travel agent or professional. However, some states and municipalities do have licensing requirements for homebased businesses, including e-commerce or internet businesses. Check with your local planning and zoning department or city/county business license department to find out if any licenses and permits are needed for your online travel business. This process will probably fall under the "least fun things to do" category because you may spend time on hold and getting the runaround, but it will save you a lot of headaches in the end.

CLICK TIP

If you start your business using equipment you already own, you may be able to deduct a portion of the cost of that equipment as a business expense on your tax return. Check with your tax advisor for guidance.

software. Other considerations are inventory, supplies, licenses, marketing, and operating capital needs (the amount of cash you need on hand to carry you until your business begins generating income). Use Figure 12.1: Startup Costs Worksheet on page 172 to help calculate how much money you're going to need.

Once you have estimated how much you need to start your business, you can then determine how much you have on hand. If you're fortunate, you will already have everything you need to get started. If you don't, now is the time to start working with the numbers and deciding what you can do without.

> ### Words of Wisdom
>
> *Successful entrepreneurs are those who analyze and minimize risk in the pursuit of profit.*
>
> —BRIAN TRACY

So, where is the money? It may be closer than you think because banks are not the only source of funds.

Personal Resources

When thinking of creative ways to come up with startup funds, do a thorough inventory of your own assets. Make a list of what you have, including savings and retirement accounts, equity in real estate, vehicles, collections, life insurance, and other investments. Though you may not want to sell your car or siphon funds from your retirement account to finance your online travel business, you may be willing to sell your collection of vintage travel posters for a few hundred dollars. But if you don't want to sell your assets for cash, think about using them as collateral for a loan.

Figure 12.1: **STARTUP COSTS WORKSHEET**

Item	Price
Office Equipment and Supplies	
Computer system	$
Printer (for computer)	
Digital camera	
Scanner	
Fax machine	
Multifunction device (fax/copier/printer/scanner)	
Copier	
Uninterruptible power supply	
Surge protector	
Calculator	
Desk	
Desk chair	
Printer stand	
Paper shredder	
File cabinet	
Bookcase	
Computer/copier paper	
Business cards	
Letterhead paper and envelopes	
Address stamp	

Figure 12.1: **STARTUP COSTS WORKSHEET,** CONTINUED

Item	Price
Office Equipment and Supplies	
Extra printer cartridge	$
Mouse pad	
Miscellaneous	
Telecommunications and Internet	
Full-featured phone system	
Voice mail	
E-mail	
Website design	
Website hosting	
High-speed internet (DSL, broadband)	
Cell phone	
Pager	
TOTAL	$

Credit Cards

Many successful businesses have been jump-started with plastic. Just be smart about it because sky-high interest rates could bury you for years. If you do use a credit card to help fund your online travel business, only charge items that will contribute to revenue generation, such as inventory and supplies.

Friends and Family

A lot of startup businesses have been funded with seed money from friends and relatives who recognized the potential value of the venture and wanted to help their loved ones succeed. However, be cautious with these arrangements; no matter how close you are, present yourself professionally, put everything in writing, and be sure the individuals you approach can afford to take the risk of investing in your business. Never accept money for a business venture from anyone who can't afford to lose that money.

Partners

Using the "strength in numbers" principle, look around for someone who may want to team up with you in your new venture. You may choose someone who has financial resources and wants to work side-by-side with you in the business. Or you may find someone who has money to invest but no interest in doing the actual work. As with your friends and family, be sure to create a written partnership agreement that clearly defines your respective responsibilities and obligations.

Government Programs

Take advantage of the abundance of local, state, and federal programs designed to support small businesses. Make your first stop the Small Business Administration (sba.gov); then investigate various other programs. Women, minorities, and veterans should check out niche financing possibilities

---

CLICK TIP

The Small Business Administration (sba.gov) recommends that businesses in general—e-commerce business owners among them—budget adequately for marketing to make sure that they are reaching potential customers. When starting a business, you should plan on spending as much as 10 percent of your expected revenue on marketing, the agency advises.

---

designed to help them get into business. The business section of your local library is a good place to begin your research.

Lending Institutions

While banks might seem like the most likely source of financing, they are generally the most conservative. Besides wanting to know exactly what the money is for (show them your e-business plan), they usually require some type of collateral such as real estate, a life insurance policy, stocks, bonds, or a savings account. If you have excellent credit, you may be able to take out a signature loan for a few thousand dollars, but the interest rate will be higher than a traditional loan.

Keep Good Records

It's important to monitor your financial progress closely and the only way you can do that is by keeping good records. You can handle the process manually; however, there are a number of excellent computer accounting programs on the market. Whatever accounting system you use will help produce financial statements that tell you exactly where you stand and what you need to do next. The key financial statements you need to understand and use regularly are:

- ➡ *Profit and loss statement.* Also called the P&L or the income statement, this statement illustrates how much your business is making or losing over a designated period—monthly, quarterly, or annually—by subtracting expenses from your revenue to arrive at a net result, which is either a profit or a loss. Initially, this document may not be of much value to you—especially during the startup phase. But over time as your profit history grows, you will appreciate this useful management tool.
- ➡ *Balance sheet.* A balance sheet is a table showing your assets, liabilities, and capital at a specific point. A balance sheet is typically generated monthly, quarterly, or annually when the books are closed.
- ➡ *Cash flow statement.* This summarizes the operating, investing, and financing activities of your business as they relate to the inflow and

outflow of cash. Its main purpose is to point out when the cash flow isn't flowing so you can work out a solution and pinpoint trouble spots in the future. As with the profit and loss statement, a cash flow statement is prepared to reflect a specific accounting period, such as monthly, quarterly, or annually.

Successful business owners review these reports regularly, at least monthly, so they always know where they stand and can quickly move to correct minor difficulties before they become major financial problems. If you wait until June to figure out whether or not you made a profit last December, you will not be in business very long.

BETTER BANKING

Some banks specialize in certain kinds of businesses or have departments that handle specific industries. You can usually tell which banks are interested in attracting loans from small businesses by their eagerness to obtain your account. Here are a few questions to ask your prospective bankers that will help you gauge their interest:

- ➡ Is it necessary to maintain certain balances before the bank will consider a loan?
- ➡ Will the bank give you a line of credit? If so, what are the requirements?
- ➡ Does the bank have limitations on the number of small loans it will grant or the types of businesses to which it will grant loans?
- ➡ What is the bank's policy regarding the size or description of checks deposited to be held for collection?
- ➡ Will checks under that size be credited immediately to your checking account balance? (This is an important question. If you don't have a previous business account to serve as a reference, some banks will hold all checks for collection until they develop experience with you. Whether the bank exercises this precaution may depend on your personal credit rating.)

12 / FINANCIAL AND BUSINESS MANAGEMENT

CLICK TIP

If you carry a balance on a credit card that is used solely for business purposes, the interest is deductible, but if you mix business and personal charges on the card, the interest is not even partially deductible.

Once you have a fiscal system in place, your next step is to open a separate checking account for your business so that you don't commingle personal and business funds. You also need a business credit card or at least a separate card in your name that you use exclusively for your online business.

Merchant Accounts

Most internet shoppers want instant gratification, which is why they prefer to pay with plastic. To be competitive in cyberspace, you must be prepared to accept debit and credit cards online. Fortunately, it's much easier to get merchant status than it has been in the past; in fact, these days merchant status providers are competing aggressively for your business.

To get a credit card merchant account, start with your own bank. Also check with various professional associations that offer merchant status as a member benefit. Most turnkey service providers offer a merchant account—for a fee. To find other online merchant account providers, type the key phrase "merchant account" in a search engine. This is a competitive industry, so shop around. It's worth taking the time to get the best deal.

Some questions you need to ask yourself (and the provider) when looking at different merchant account options are:

➡ *What are the requirements for opening a merchant account?* (Find out in advance what type of documentation the provider needs, including EIN number, credit check, website information, copy of your business license, etc.)

➡ *What are the costs and fees associated with a merchant account?* (Costs vary from one provider to the next, as do the transaction fees. Find out in advance what the fees are for processing, maintenance, transactions, etc.)

➡ *What are their rate review policies?* (In the beginning it's difficult to determine what your monthly sales volume will be. Find out if your merchant account provider is willing to review your account periodically and lower your discount rate if you are producing a higher volume in sales.)

PAYPAL

PayPal (paypal.com) allows you to accept credit card, bank account, and PayPal account balance payments over the internet. This is a fast, easy, secure way for people to exchange funds online. Depending on your sales volume, PayPal offers several different solutions for merchants, including shopping cart integration and checkout on your site or through PayPal.

PayPal offers a variety of reporting and management tools, including detailed history logs and monthly account statements. You can also automatically include shipping and sales tax during checkout, and print shipping labels and postage with just a few keystrokes. Another reason for its popularity is that PayPal offers a Seller Protection Policy that protects sellers against chargebacks.

Although PayPal is free to customers, as an online seller you must have a Premier or Business account so that you can accept credit cards as well as bank payments (sellers are charged a small fee to receive funds). PayPal charges two fees: the standard rate, which is 2.9 percent plus 30 cents per transaction, and the merchant rate, which is between 1.9 percent and 2.5 percent plus 30 cents per transaction. The qualification for the merchant rate is $3,000 per month in sales volume.

Some of PayPal's Premier Account benefits include the ability to receive any type of payment, including credit cards, for low fees; access to an exclusive customer service hotline; and use of special sellers tools. With a Business Account, you can use all the features of a Premier Account, have multiple logins, and do business under a corporate name.

WARNING

Businesses lose more than $1 billion annually because of bad checks, so if you decide to accept them, check the date for accuracy (do not accept a check that is undated, postdated, or more than 30 days old) and be sure the written amount and numerical amount agree.

➡ *Have you carefully read everything associated with this merchant account?* (This includes all agreements and contracts. Before signing up with a provider make sure you understand the terms, length of contract, and fees associated with this account.)

Taxing Matters

Businesses are required to pay a wide range of taxes, and there are no exceptions for businesses that sell online. Keep good records so you can offset your local, state and federal income taxes with your operating expenses. If you have employees, you'll be responsible for payroll taxes. If you operate as a corporation, you'll have to pay payroll taxes for yourself; as a sole proprietor, you'll pay self-employment tax. Then there are property taxes, taxes on your equipment and inventory, fees and taxes to maintain your corporate status, your business license fee (which is really a tax), and other lesser-known taxes. Take the time to review all your tax liabilities with your accountant.

A homebased business offers substantial tax breaks, but you must be sure your setup meets IRS requirements. To take the home office deduction, you must have a room that is used solely as your office and/or workroom. It cannot be the corner of your family room, nor can the office do double-duty as a den or guest room.

What can you deduct? Directly related expenses, which are those that benefit only the business part of your home, and a portion of indirect expenses, which are the costs involved in keeping up and running your entire home. For example, your office furniture and equipment are fully deductible as directly related expenses. In the area of indirect expenses, you may deduct a portion of your

CLICK TIP

The travel and tourism industry generates $100 billion in tax revenue for local, state, and federal governments each year, according to statistics from the Travel Industry Association. Without those tax revenues, each household in the United States would see its tax bill rise by $898.

household utilities and services (electric, gas, water, sewage, trash collection, etc.) based on the percentage of space you use for business purposes. Other examples of indirect expenses include real estate taxes, deductible mortgage interest, casualty losses, rent, insurance, repairs, security systems, and depreciation.

Sales Tax

A potentially sticky area for online business owners is sales tax. Many large retailers with online operations have begun collecting sales tax on their internet sales, and legislation affecting how internet sales are taxed is pending at state and federal levels. As a business owner, you are responsible for knowing the law and doing the right thing. Talk to your accountant or contact your state's revenue service, and be sure you clearly understand the rules as they apply to your business.

Sales tax is generally paid on products that you sell, whereas, tax on travel bookings and reservations is added on by the travel supplier, such as the cruise line or airline. To charge and collect sales tax, you'll need a sales tax ID number (sometimes referred to as a reseller's permit). This is usually a very simple process; just check with your state's department of revenue for information on how to proceed.

To learn more abut internet sales tax, visit the following webites:

➡ *The Sales Tax Institute (salestaxinstitute.com)*—provides a range of services and links associated with sales tax.
➡ *DavidHardesty.com*—provides news and feature articles about e-commerce taxation, including e-mail updates from e-commerce expert David Hardesty.

> **WARNING**
>
> Report your income from online sales on your tax return no matter how insignificant you think it is. Remember that failing to report income is a crime. Also, be sure to take any deductions to which you are entitled.

➡ *Streamlined Sales Tax Governing Board (streamlinedsalestax.org)*—offers up-to-date information and news abut the SSUTA.

Business Classifications

For tax purposes you will need to define your online travel business to the Internal Revenue Service. What goes into choosing a legal structure? If you're starting the business by yourself, you'll be the one making all of the decisions. However, if other people are involved, you need to consider the issue of asset protection and limiting your financial liability in the event things don't go well. There are several types of business classifications to choose from, each with benefits and drawbacks.

Sole Proprietorship

Many homebased cyberpreneurs prefer to be classified as sole proprietors, at least initially, though it's not unusual for a business owner to change that status to include a partner or incorporate the company as the business grows. The beauty of sole proprietorship is its simplicity. There's not a lot to do in the way of paperwork and filing fees. But the disadvantage of being a sole proprietor is that if anything goes wrong (i.e., you are sued or default on a loan), creditors can go after your personal assets.

Partnership

When two or more people go into business together, a partnership is formed. Just make sure you have a well-written agreement in place. A partnership works basically like a sole proprietorship, except the partners share in the profits, expenses, and liabilities of the business. Chris Lopinto, co-founder of

ExpertFlyer.com, strongly supports the idea of forming a partnership with one or more individuals who have complimentary skills to yours. "If you're good in sales, partner with someone who's good in technical, or better at running a business," he advises.

Limited Liability Company (LLC)

This type of structure has a lot of the same elements as a partnership or corporation, but it can reduce the partners' or shareholders' potential liability.

S Corporation

An S Corporation provides tax benefits to owners because they only pay taxes on their own income from the S Corporation. Although this structure offers all of the legal and financial protection that a traditional corporation does, it does not have to pay taxes on its corporate income.

Incorporation

Typically, a corporation is comprised of shareholders who elect a director, who nominates officers, who then hire employees to manage and operate the company. But it's entirely possible for a corporation to have only one shareholder and function essentially as a sole proprietorship. The biggest advantage of forming a corporation is in the area of asset protection, making sure the assets you don't want to put into the business don't stand liable for the debt of the business.

Is any one of these business structures better than another? What's important is what's best for you. Consider what you want to do now, and where you expect to take your company. Then choose the form that is most appropriate for your particular needs.

People You Should Know

As a business owner, you may be the boss, but you can't be expected to know everything. There are going to be times and situations when you'll need to turn to other professionals for information and assistance. The professional service providers you're likely to need consist of the following.

Accountant

Whether directly or indirectly, your accountant most likely has the greatest impact on the success or failure of your business. A good accountant will always be aware of the ever-changing tax laws and how they apply to your business. He can counsel you on tax issues if you are forming a corporation as well as advise what types of business deductions you are eligible for.

Attorney

Look for a lawyer who practices in the area of business law, has a good reputation, and values your patronage. An attorney can help you collect bad debts and establish personnel policies and procedures. And whenever you are unsure of the legal ramifications of any situation, call your attorney immediately.

Insurance Agent

A good independent insurance agent can assist you with all aspects of your business insurance, from general liability to workers' compensation, and probably even handle your personal lines as well. Look for an agent who works with a wide range of insurers and understands your particular business.

Banker

In addition to a business bank account, you should have a good relationship with a banker. The bank you've always done your personal banking with may not necessarily be the best bank for your business. Talk to several bankers before making a decision on where to place your business.

Other Experts

As your business grows you may find the need to seek the services of other professionals in various, related fields. A business consultant can help you evaluate your business plan; a marketing consultant can assist you with marketing strategies; and a human resources consultant can teach you how to avoid costly mistakes when you are ready to hire employees. There is also the computer expert who can help you maintain, troubleshoot and expand your system as needed, while a web designer can develop a professional looking site for your business.

No matter how good you are at what you do, chances are you can't do it all—and you shouldn't. So find ways to network and get in touch with professionals who can help you make your business a success.

What's in the Forecast?

You don't need a crystal ball to predict future revenue, but you do need a formula to foresee how much you can expect to make in the weeks, months, and years ahead, because these numbers will become your sales goals. Use Figure 12.2: Projected Income and Operating Expenses Worksheet below to help you work out a formula.

Also, pay close attention to and utilize your key financial statements on a routine basis. Plan for the costs of growth and watch for signs of developing problems so you can figure out how to best deal with them before they turn into a major crisis. Developing analytical foresight demonstrates that you are an astute business owner on top of every situation.

Figure 12.2: **PROJECTED INCOME AND OPERATING EXPENSES**

Some of the items will not apply, and you may have additional anticipated monthly income and expenditures to add.

	Expenses	Income
Projected Monthly Income		$
Monthly income from tours		
Monthly income from product sales		
Monthly income from affiliate sales		
Other monthly income:		
Total Projected Monthly Income		$

Figure 12.2: **PROJECTED INCOME AND OPERATING EXPENSES,** CONTINUED

	Expenses	Income
Projected Monthly Operating Expenses	$	
Rent (if commercial location)		
Utilities		
Phone		
Cell phone		
Accounting and legal fees		
Advertising and promotion		
Loan repayment		
Bank charges		
Insurance		
Credit card commissions		
Reference materials/subscription renewals		
Postage		
Web hosting		
Internet service provider		
High speed internet (DSL, Broadband)		
Office supplies		
Products/inventory (for sale)		
Travel expenses		
Host agency fees		
Miscellaneous		
Total Projected Monthly Expenses	$	
Projected Net Monthly Income		$

Chapter 13

Delivering First-Class Customer Service

*G*reat customer service is essential for an online business owner to be successful. The internet has changed the face of online travel and e-commerce in countless ways, but it still hasn't "changed everything," as we so often hear—certainly not when it comes to good old-fashioned customer service.

E-tailers need to understand that what keeps those virtual doors open is a firm commitment to customer satisfaction— the level of quality, responsiveness, integrity, and timeliness that makes today's client a repeat customer. You want customers to keep coming back because not only is it good for business, it's also a good business practice in and of itself. Part of this process includes establishing a refund and return policy in case something is wrong, dealing with difficult customers, and effectively communicating with buyers so transactions have a happy ending.

How to Provide Great Customer Service

Whether your business is selling from a website, a brick-and-mortar store, or both, the basic principles of customer service remain the same:

- → *See your business through your customers' eyes.* Is your operation user-friendly, efficient, and responsive?
- → *Ask what your customers want and need.* Don't assume that you know what your customers want; ask them—and listen to their answers.
- → *Meet or exceed expectations.* When you promise to do something—whether it's to provide information, ship a product, or something else—do as you promised, or better.
- → *Ask if there's anything else you can do.* When the transaction is complete, find out if you can provide any other product or service. A simple, "Is there anything else I can help you with?" can net you additional sales and invaluable goodwill.
- → *Keep in touch.* Let your customers know that they are important to you after the sale is complete and you've gotten their money.

> ### Words of Wisdom
>
> *We can believe that we know where the world should go. But unless we're in touch with our customers, our model of the world can diverge from reality. There's no substitute for innovation, of course, but innovation is no substitute for being in touch, either.*
>
> —STEVE BALLMER, CHIEF EXECUTIVE OFFICER OF MICROSOFT CORPORATION

- → *Be a copycat.* Pay attention to good customer service when you receive it, whether it's in a restaurant, the grocery store, or elsewhere, and duplicate those techniques in your own operation.

Communication Is the Key

Make it easy for customers to communicate with you if they have a problem, concern, or question. Post contact information such as your e-mail, phone, and fax numbers in prominent places on your website. You may even want to have a specific web page for contact information.

Another way to make yourself accessible to customers is by providing a live chat program on your site so that customers can have quick access to you when asking questions. This can be done by integrating your website with software specially designed for live chats like BoldChat (boldchat.com). Or you can sign up with an AOL Instant Messenger account (aol.com) so that visitors can talk to you whenever you are online.

Treat all your communications with online buyers as business correspondence, and remember that the structure, tone, and details of your e-mails are a strong reflection of your operation. Begin your e-mails with a salutation, write in complete sentences, end with a proper closing, and proofread and spell-check; then proofread again before you hit "send." Respond to communications as quickly as possible so as not to leave customers hanging. The faster you respond, the more they will be impressed.

If you see a pattern in the types of questions you get asked, look for ways to answer them on your website's FAQ page or in a Help section. These are good for answering common questions customers frequently have; plus, it saves them the trouble of having to contact you and wait for a reply. You can also develop standard responses that you can easily paste into an e-mail and quickly customize for the particular situation.

CLICK TIP

Let your customers tell others what they think by posting their comments on your website. It's been proven that unbiased online reviews carry a lot more weight than most other forms of marketing communication. Tools to help you get started are Power Reviews (power reviews.com) or Prospero Community CM (prospero.com).

Prickly People

Some customers are difficult because that's their basic nature, but others may give you a hard time simply because they don't know any better. Sometimes a newcomer may need a little hand-holding, but think of it as an opportunity. If you take the time to nurture their online learning experience and guide them through the process, they (and their friends) may become loyal customers. Another reason why good communications are critical.

Try not to take it personally when customers are rude and excessively demanding. Not every transaction is going to go smoothly. The important thing to remember is to remain cool, calm, and professional—but not so much that you seem detached. When working out a resolution with a customer, offer him more than one alternative, if possible. Sometimes what may seem like the obvious solution is not what the customer had in mind. Providing options can go a long way toward smoothing ruffled feathers because the customer feels that you care about resolving his issues.

Policies and Procedures

Establish a comprehensive set of policies and procedures to protect you, your clients, transportation and lodging providers, and the various other entities involved in delivering travel services. The specific issues you need to address will vary depending on the type of travel service you offer.

Before your clients make a reservation, be sure they understand your cancellation policies and know what is required to receive a full or partial refund, as well as when no refund will be made.

CLICK TIP

Review your website and policies to be sure the text is consistent. For example, your website should not give customers a 30-day cancellation period if your policies state they must cancel at least 60 days in advance for a refund.

Include a "hold harmless" disclaimer in your contract that states that you are not liable or responsible for any loss, damage, injury, accident, delays, or cancellations caused by acts of God or the actions of third parties.

Reserve the right to refuse or cancel your services to anyone you feel may impede the welfare or enjoyment of other members in the tour. If there is concern about someone's health, that is, mental or physical condition, you can also reserve the right to refuse or cancel your services. Just be sure you do it fairly and without discriminating.

Will You Take Returns?

Customer returns are inevitable, even for the most conscientious cyberpreneur. Buying online is a gamble, and buyers feel more reassured if they have the option of returning the item under certain circumstances. Decide how you're going to deal with returns and state that policy clearly on your website and on invoices.

Your return policy should include a time limit, a description of the circumstances under which items can be returned, who pays for shipping (Will you refund shipping costs if an item is returned? Some e-tailers don't.), whether or not you charge a restocking fee, and any procedures customers must follow to return an item. If your return policy promises to make refunds to dissatisfied customers, you are required by federal law to do that.

STELLAR CUSTOMER SERVICE: DO YOU HAVE WHAT IT TAKES?

The great thing about the internet is that anyone can set up shop. Of course, that also means you now have to compete with the big guys—and customer service is no exception. "Customers today are very savvy," says Lauren Freedman, president of the e-tailing group inc., an e-commerce consulting firm in Chicago. "They expect best-of-breed customer service everywhere they shop on the web. They don't care if you are smaller."

STELLAR CUSTOMER SERVICE:
DO YOU HAVE WHAT IT TAKES?, CONTINUED

Each year, Freedman's firm tracks the top 100 e-tailers on 11 criteria relative to customer service and communication. The most successful online businesses offer the following:

1. *A toll-free number.* "This is pretty critical today," says Freedman. "If a small business doesn't offer this now, it should think about it."

2. *Keyword search.* According to Freedman, "People today are used to searching for things online, and they want a seamless search experience on the websites they are considering buying from."

3. *Time answers to e-mail questions.* "A small e-tailer should probably strive for 48 hours," says Freedman, who adds it's important to personally address customer queries vs. sending automated responses.

4. *Four or fewer days to receive a package via ground shipping.* "A small e-tailer should try to strive for five business days," says Freedman. "And they should make it very clear—in all their communications with their customers—what their shipping policies are."

5. *Six or fewer clicks to checkout.*

6. *Inventory status.* While real-time status is best, "[Let] your customer know within 24 hours if the product they are ordering is in stock or is not in stock," says Freedman.

7. *Online shipping status.* "[Offer] a link to UPS or FedEx so they can check their orders on their sites," says Freedman.

8. *Order confirmation in the shipping cart.*

9. *An e-mail order confirmation with the order number included.*

10. *Recommendations for other products and features during the shopping process.* "This is a standard for the larger merchants, but something that small e-merchants should strive for," says Freedman, who adds doing so can help you increase order size.

11. *Clearly displayed customer service hours.* "This is especially important if you have limited customer service hours," says Freedman.

Source: Melissa Campanelli's *Open an Online Business in 10 Days* (Entrepreneur Press, 2007)

Chapter 14

Successful Online Travel Entrepreneurs

*B*y now, you should know how to get started and have a good idea of what to do, and what not to do, in your online travel business. While it is true that you learn things by doing them, another way to learn something new is by example. Throughout the book, our featured travel entrepreneurs have shared their advice and insight, because nothing teaches as well as the voice of experience. After all, there's no reason you should repeat the mistakes of others if they're willing to tell you about them first. Now it's time to meet these folks, find out how they got started, and hear a few more words of wisdom . . .

Expert Flyer

(expertflyer.com)

Approximately four years ago, Chris Lopinto, co-founder of ExpertFlyer.com, and his partner created a niche in the travel industry specifically with the frequent flyer in mind. "Basically, we sell access to information that usually only travel agents can see," says Lopinto. "These are seasoned business travelers who want more in-depth, nitty-gritty, unbiased information about travel arrangements."

Lopinto says the concept for this innovative site came from his own personal experience as well as his partner's, a retired airline captain who flies 150,000 miles a year. "We realized there was a need for more in-depth information than the Expedia or Travelocity type sites were providing, so we found a way to get access to the same airline reservation systems that travel agents do."

ExpertFlyer.com uses a subscription-based model that provides subscribers with pertinent information they cannot find anywhere else. This unique airline information tool helps busy travelers find tickets, upgrades, preferred seating, and provides up-to-the-minute statistics about arrivals and departures for all of the airlines. When the requested information becomes available, subscribers can choose to be notified via cell phone, PDA, or computer.

Lopinto advises online travel entrepreneurs to find something in the industry they would personally like to see changed or different. "My number-one tip is to find something that is applicable to you," he advises.

> ## Words of Wisdom
>
> *As you begin to take action toward the fulfillment of your goals and dreams, you must realize that not every action will be perfect. Not every action will produce the desired result. Not every action will work. Making mistakes, getting it almost right, and experimenting to see what happens are all part of the process of eventually getting it right.*
>
> —JACK CANFIELD, INSPIRATIONAL SELF-HELP AUTHOR
> AND SUCCESS COACH

"Then think about how to bring that concept to reality. If you go under the assumption that other people feel the same way, there's your market."

Man Tripping and Chick Vacations

(mantripping.com; chickvacations.com)

James Hill was a writer for washingtonpost.com's Entertainment Guide from 2001–2003, before going to work as a marketing director for a manufacturer in Chicago. Then, he and his wife, Heather, decided to start an Integrated Online Marketing firm (marketinghelpnet.com), which they still successfully manage today.

About a year ago James started to miss writing so he and Heather did some research and saw that "girl getaways" was a unique concept. "Although there was quite a bit of competition, we still felt it provided the ability to write unique articles that would fit into that mold," says James. They put together a list of subjects to write about to attract people and keep them coming back— and Chick Vacations (chickvacations.com) was launched. In addition to providing quality content for its readers, Chick Vacations also has a travel concierge service where Heather helps women plan their getaways.

"After working with Heather and listening to her ideas I started thinking about 'guy getaways' and how to approach that market, too," says James. So it wasn't long afterwards that the Man Tripping blog (mantripping.com) was created to help guys plan their "mancations."

James admits that anyone can start an online business in a day, although he would not recommend it. "You really need to think about what you want to do, what your goals are, who your competitors are, and how you're going to make money with this business," he advises. "Additionally, think about your exit strategy. Do you want to turn a hobby into a full-time gig? Build up a business and then sell it? Know these things before you get started."

> ## Words of Wisdom
>
> *In business, I've discovered that my purpose is to do my best to my utmost ability every day. That's my standard. I learned early in my life that I had high standards.*
>
> —Donald Trump

My Trip Journal

(mytripjournal.com)

In 2001, Dan Parlow and his wife took their two young boys to China for three months. As they traveled, they kept family and friends updated about their whereabouts using an online map and updated journal entries. "After returning from our trip we received a lot of feedback from people who had been reading our journal as we traveled," says Parlow. "That's when we got the idea of making a business out of it."

From there, Parlow's family started My Trip Journal (mytripjournal.com) in a joint venture with partners who knew how to handle all the programming, mapping, and everything else. Parlow says it took a couple of years for the site to be completely developed, so it didn't actually go live until early 2004.

Initially, My Trip Journal was developed as a subscription site that offered a free trial period of 30 days before members had to pay the subscription fee. "In mid-2007, at the request of some of our partners we custom brand for, we basically had the opportunity to reach broader markets if we created a free version that was supported by advertising," says Parlow. "Now, instead of having a free trial and a paid version, we have a free advertising supported version, and a premium paid version as well. The latter has a number of additional features plus no ads if you and your friends or families are viewing it."

> ## Words of Wisdom
>
> *The number-one benefit of information technology is that it empowers people to do what they want to do. It lets people be creative. It lets people be productive. It lets people learn things they didn't think they could learn before, and so in a sense it is all about potential.*
>
> —STEVE BALLMER, CHIEF EXECUTIVE OFFICER, MICROSOFT CORPORATION

New York Outdoors

(newyorkoutdoors.wordpress.com)

Sue Freeman, an avid outdoors enthusiast and travel guidebook writer, started her popular blog New York Outdoors for several reasons, with marketing as the biggest motive. "The primary purpose of the blog is to promote our

14 travel guidebooks and provide information about local trails and outdoor events around Central and Western New York," she says. "However, I try not to get heavy with the sales part of it because I personally don't like that kind of strategy."

When she and husband, Rich, first created the website (footprint press.com) to sell the guidebooks, they sent out an e-newsletter to subscribers on a mailing list once a month for 10 years—until last summer. "That's when I decided to convert the newsletter to a blog because we were having problems with spam rejections and other publication issues," she says. Now, Freeman believes she is reaching a much wider audience by going with a blog. "I find there is a lot more interconnectivity with the World Wide Web. People looking for certain topics are much more likely to find an article on my blog, which means more exposure."

While they were marketing their guidebooks, Rich and Sue would ask related stores, such as bike shops, to display their guidebooks near the cash register for more visibility. However, they had a hard time finding stands to display the books that didn't have to be bought in bulk at a reasonable price, so Rich made some. People began asking about the stands, and they started selling them online (displaystands4you.com) all over the world. They have since developed nine different models that are sold to schools, writers, museums, chefs, coffee shops, and anyone else needing a quality, low-cost display stand.

> ## Words of Wisdom
>
> *The price of success is hard work, dedication to the job at hand, and the determination that whether we win or lose, we have applied the best of ourselves to the task at hand.*
>
> —VINCE LOMBARDI, FOOTBALL COACH AND MOTIVATIONAL TEACHER

Our Cruise Planner

(ourcruiseplanner.com)

Jenny Reed, who lives near Atlanta, Georgia, is a cruise and group travel specialist. Seven years ago she and her husband decided to take their passion for traveling and buy a franchise from Cruise Planners. "I was supposed to start my training through the franchise on September 12, 2001," she recalls. "But with the tragic events of September 11, that didn't happen until November." Looking back, Reed feels that for anyone to launch a business during those turbulent and economically shaky times, especially a travel business, was a huge risk. But seven years later they are still going strong. "After living through that, I feel there is no challenge that cannot be done," she says.

As part their franchise agreement, Reed is required to stay up-to-date on her training. Fortunately, Cruise Planners does an excellent job of providing continuing education for its members. "We can do webinars with the cruise lines that are customized specifically for our agents. Everything is virtual, and we don't have to actually travel somewhere for a conference." However, Reed enjoys it when her franchise holds seminars at sea, which they do throughout the year. "You get to have a little play with a little bit of work," she says. "Plus it's a great way to network with other business owners."

> ## Words of Wisdom
>
> *If you have a task to perform and are vitally interested in it, excited and challenged by it, then you will exert maximum energy. But in the excitement, the pain of fatigue dissipates, and the exuberance of what you hope to achieve overcomes the weariness.*
>
> —JIMMY CARTER, FORMER PRESIDENT OF THE UNITED STATES OF AMERICA

Reed says that Cruise Planners prides itself on being a company that stays on the cutting edge by constantly educating its agents. "Keeping up with the cruise lines, along with the rules and regulations, is a pretty big challenge because everything is constantly changing in the travel industry."

The best advice that Reed would give people considering an online travel business is to carefully research the specialty area they want to get into because the industry is very competitive. "This should not be a make-money-quick type of business," Reed cautions. "And don't be afraid to ask questions—lots of questions."

Steele Luxury Travel

(steeletravel.com)

Steele Luxury Travel is a brand new concept in group travel. The owner, Dane Steele Green, has traveled all over the world and saw there was a definite need in the travel marketplace for the lesbian, gay, transsexual, and transgender community. "These people travel all the time," he says. "Many of my brothers and sisters, if you will, don't have families or offspring, but they do have a lot of disposable income and they travel fabulously!" So he created Steele Luxury Travel as a travel company that caters to the gay community, going to exotic, upscale destinations that are very popular throughout the world.

Currently, Steele Luxury Travel is planning five vacation packages to four gay-friendly destinations that are fully customizable and tailored to the individual tastes of each traveler. "Joe and Ron can go to our website and add anything from tango lessons to golf lessons to touring the back artists' gallery of Buenos Aires," says Green. "Pick when you want to go. Do what you love to do. We'll take care of the rest, including picking you up in a Mercedes Benz. It's all about luxury."

Prior to starting his own travel business, Green worked in marketing for several airlines, including Jet Blue, which he feels helped to prepare him for this line of work. "When starting a travel company, you need to know how to acclimate to various people," he says. "You have to know how people think, how people work, how people travel. Apply those skills to a niche market and you're in business."

Green feels very blessed that his travel company has taken off so successfully and contributes at least 5 percent of the company's profits to different charities. "It's very important to me. I feel that in order to make a company work you have to give back to the community before they give to you,"

> ## Words of Wisdom
>
> *I have learned the novice can often see things that the expert overlooks. All that is necessary is not to be afraid of making mistakes, or of appearing naive.*
>
> —ABRAHAM MASLOW, PSYCHOLOGIST AND WRITER

he says. "It also works hand in hand. When people see you're donating to charity, they want to work with you. They feel good about what you're doing."

Viva Travels

(vivatravels.com)

Before launching her custom guided and self-guided bicycle tours business Viva Travels in 2004, Jennifer Sage had been in the fitness industry for 18 years, with an MBA in International Management. In 1988, she rode her bike solo around Europe, and then lived in France for a year. "I began working for luxury bicycle tour companies in 1989, and returned almost every summer to organize and lead tours." This gave her many years of experience in the cycling industry as well as an excellent understanding of the ins and outs of cycling in Europe. "I often thought, 'Hmmm, I could do this just as good or even better!'" And so she did.

The year her travel site was launched, Sage says she was lucky to have a phenomenon like Lance Armstrong help drive traffic to her site, through very little effort on her part. "I know I wouldn't have done as well that first year otherwise, because I hadn't done enough research on where my target market was. I can honestly say I winged my advertising and didn't have a concrete plan."

Sage's advice to newcomers in the travel industry is to define the demographics and psychographics of your target market very well—and do your market research! "Determine who your ideal client is and market directly to him/her/them," she advises. "Who is your competition? What are they doing to find their ideal clients?"

> ## Words of Wisdom
>
> *In all realms of life it takes courage to stretch your limits, express your power, and fulfill your potential . . . it's no different in the financial realm.*
>
> —SUZE ORMAN, PERSONAL FINANCE AUTHOR AND MEDIA PERSONALITY

Wanderlust and Lipstick

(wanderlustandlipstick.com)

Beth Whitman of Wanderlust and Lipstick has been a self-described "travel addict" and solo traveler for more than 20 years. Early in her travels she found that women in general are very fearful about traveling, especially on their own, so she started teaching workshops at various universities to encourage and inspire them to be more adventurous and plan their own excursions.

About a year ago, she published her first book, *Wanderlust and Lipstick: The Essential Guide for Women Traveling Solo,* and this year will release two more books under the Wanderlust and Lipstick series: *For Women Traveling to India* and *For Women Traveling with Children.*

Like any other entrepreneur, Whitman has always had the burning desire to work for herself and knew that it would have to be in the travel industry because that was the one thing she was so passionate about. For many years she was unsure how to make her dream a reality until the World Wide Web showed her the possibilities. "The internet has opened up so many more opportunities for people," she says. "I don't know if I could have had a successful business five or ten years ago, but today you can definitely do it. It really makes sense because you can reach so many people and be creative about it. I've got access to the entire world at this point."

Whitman wants new business owners to understand this is not a quick and easy process. "Sure, you can easily get set up with a site or blog," she says. "But it takes a little bit of work every single day to build up your audience."

She says that if she had to do it all over again, it would be on a smaller scale. "I bit off a lot with my website when I first got started, and at times I have felt it has been totally unmanageable," she says. "There are so many pieces to my website that I ended up making it really complicated. I would recommend to someone doing this today to start smaller and add on pieces as they grow."

Words of Wisdom

Learning is an active process. We learn by doing. Only knowledge that is used sticks in your mind.

—Dale Carnegie, Self-Development Author and Trainer

Internet Resource Guide

*T*hey say you can never be too rich or too young. While these could be argued, I believe "You can never have too many resources." Therefore, I present for your consideration a wealth of sources for you to check into, check out, and harness for your own personal information blitz.

These sources are tidbits, ideas to get you started on your research. They are by no means the only sources out there, and they should not be taken as the ultimate answer. I have done my research, but businesses do tend to move, change, fold, and expand. As I have repeatedly stressed, do your homework. Get out and start investigating.

Advertising Campaigns

Google AdWords
adwords.google.com

Google AdSense
google.com/adsense

MSN
advertising.microsoft.com/ad-programs

Quantcast Internet Ratings Service
quantcast.com
This is a free service that provides audience profiles for millions of websites. A useful tool if you want to look up specific sites for advertising purposes or want to list your site so that advertisers can find you.

Travel Ad Network (TAN)
traveladnetwork.com

Yahoo!
sem.smallbusiness.yahoo.com/searchenginemarketing/

Yahoo! Publisher Network
publisher.yahoo.com

Affiliate Programs

Affiliate Classroom
affiliateclassroom.com/resources/travel.php

All Affiliates
allaffiliateprograms.com/travel_27/

Associate Programs
associateprograms.com

Commission Junction
cj.com

Home Based Travel Affiliate
HomeBasedTravelAffiliate.com

LinkShare
linkshare.com

My Affiliate Program
myaffiliateprogram.com

The Pepperjam Network
pepperjamnetwork.com

Refer-It
refer-it.com

Affiliate Programs for Travel Sites
Air Travel

AirGorilla (airgorilla.com/help/affiliates.html)
Commission: $10 per airline reservation
Merchant managed

Alaska Airlines (alaskaair.com)
Commission: $2 per airline ticket
Managed by Performics (performics.com)

Delta (delta.com/about_delta/partnering_with_delta)
Tiered commission structure: $3–$5 per qualified transaction
Managed by LinkShare.com

Economy Travel (economytravel.com/affiliate.html)
Commission: $20 per international reservation; $4 per domestic reservation
Managed by Commission Junction (cj.com)

Hotels

Hotel Club (affiliates.hotelclub.com)
Commission: 50 percent of total net booking
Merchant managed

Hotels Combined (hotelscombined.com/Affiliates.aspx)
Commissions vary
Merchant managed

Starwood Hotels (starwoodhotels.com/westin/affiliate/index.html)
Commission: 2 percent on every booking
Managed by Commission Junction (cj.com)

Wyndham Hotels (roadtraveler.com/RoadTraveler/control/affiliate)
Commission: 3 percent on all bookings
Managed by LinkShare.com

Car Rentals

Alamo Car Rental (alamo.com/affiliates.do)
Commission: 3 percent and up
Merchant managed

Budget Rent a Car
(budget.com/budgetWeb/html/en/aboutus/partners/affiliates/index.html)
Commission: 3 percent on completed rentals
Merchant managed

Enterprise (enterpriseaffiliate.com)
Commission: up to 2.5 percent
Managed by LinkShare.com

Cruises

1 Cruise (1cruise.com/affiliates.html)
Commissions vary
Merchant managed

Cruise Direct (cruisedirectonline.com/becomeatravelpartner.htm)
Commission: 2 percent
Merchant managed

Vacation Consultants of America (vcatravel.com/affiliate_services.asp)
Commissions vary
Merchant managed

All-Inclusive (air, hotel, car, etc.)

Montrose Travel (montrosetravel.com/afflink_program.html)
Three different affiliate or partner rewards programs to choose from

Priceline (priceline.com/affiliates)
Commissions vary by product
Managed by Commission Junction (cj.com)

Travelocity (travelocity.com)
Commissions: flat commissions on airline and cruise reservations; revenue
    share on car rentals, hotel bookings, and packages
Merchant managed

Travel/Trip Insurance

AIG Travel Guard (buy.travelguard.com/tgdirect/info/affiliateprogram.aspx)
Commissions vary
Managed by Commission Junction (cj.com)

Insure My Trip (insuremytrip.com/partners-1000-0-0-43.html)
Commission: $10 per referral
Merchant managed

Travel Insurance Center
(travelinsurancecenter.com/eng/affiliates/aff_registration/home.cfm)
Commissions vary
Merchant managed

Travel Tools

ECTACO Electronic Calendars (ectaco.com/partnership)
Commissions vary
Merchant managed

InfoHub (infohub.com/scripts/html_cgi/affiliate/aff_overview.html)
Commission: $2 per (free) brochure
Merchant managed

Maps.com (maps.com/AffiliateProgram.aspx)
Commission: up to 12 percent
Managed by Commission Junction (cj.com)

Miscellaneous Affiliate Programs

Affiliate Classroom (affiliateclassroom.com/resources/travel.php)

All Affiliates (allaffiliateprograms.com/travel_27/)

Commission Junction (cj.com)

Home Based Travel Affiliate (HomeBasedTravelAffiliate.com) Note: Book purchase required for access to site

LinkShare (linkshare.com)

My Affiliate Program (myaffiliateprogram.com)

Article Directories

A1 Articles
a1articles.com

Article Dashboard
articledashboard.com

Author Connection
authorconnection.com

e-Topic
e-topic.com

Ezine Articles
ezinearticles.com

GoArticles
goarticles.com

HubPages
hubpages.com

Idea Marketers
ideamarketers.com

iSnare
isnare.com

Search Warp
searchwarp.com

Squidoo
squidoo.com

WikiHow
wikihow.com

Autoresponders and E-Newsletter Services

Aweber
aweber.com

Bronto
bronto.com

Campaigner
campaigner.com

Constant Contact
constantcontact.com

Exact Target
exacttarget.com

GetResponse
getresponse.com

iContact
icontact.com

iMakeNews
imakenews.com

PGI Connect
premiereglobal.com

Blogging Platforms and Aggregators

Blog Carnival
blogcarnival.com/bc/

BlogExplosion
blogexplosion.com

Blogger
blogger.com

BlogRolling
blogrolling.com

Eponym
eponym.com

LifeType
lifetype.com

Movable Type
sixapart.com/movabletype

Technorati
technorati.com

TypePad
typepad.com

WebLogs
weblogs.com

WordPress.com
wordpress.com

WordPress.org
wordpress.org

Computer Security

Acronis True Image 11 Home
acronis.com

Genie Backup Manager
genie-soft.com

Scambusters
scambusters.org

Symantec's GoBack
symantec.com

Symantec's Norton Ghost 12.0
symantec.com

Digital Certificates (SSL)

GeoTrust
geotrust.com

Network Solutions
networksolutions.com

Thawte
thawte.com

Trustwave
trustwave.com

VeriSign
verisign.com

Domain Registation and Web Hosting

Bravenet
bravenet.com
Complete web host packages and domain registration.

GoDaddy
godaddy.com
Full service web solutions: domains, web hosting, site building, and SSL certificates.

Nameboy
nameboy.com
Nickname generator and domain name registration.

NameStormers
namestormers.com
Name finding service.

NetFirms
netfirms.com
Web hosting, domain name, e-commerce, e-mail, e-marketing services and
technology solutions.

Register.com
register.com
Domain registration, web hosting, and e-mail services.

Sedo.com
sedo.com
Buy and sell expired domain names.

SnapNames
snapnames.com
Buy and sell expired domain names.

File Transfer Protocol (FTP) Services

CuteFTP
cuteftp.com

Ipswitch
ipswitch.com

Internet Research

Forrester Research, Inc.
forrester.com
An independent technology and market research company

Fuld & Co.'s Internet Intelligence Index
fuld.com
Research and consulting firm in the field of business and competitive intelligence. Has links to more than 600 intelligence-related internet sites.

Hoover's
hoovers.com
Provides valuable business intelligence including company information, business news, and more. General information can be accessed for free. Subscribers can take advantage of additional content and tools like executive bios, lead generation tools, and company histories.

KnowX
knowx.com
Free and fee-based background information about businesses, people, and assets.

Thomas Register
thomasnet.com
Get supplier information for a variety of travel products.

Online Travel Resources

Away.com
away.com
Great travel ideas and all the tools to get you there.

Business Travel News Online
btnmag.com/businesstravelnews/index.jsp
News resource for business and corporate travel planners.

GORP.com
gorp.away.com
Comprehensive National Park information and recommendations.

Lonely Planet
lonelyplanet.com
World's largest online guidebook site with excellent quality of destination
   information.

Sabre Travel Network
sabretravelnetwork.com
Travel agency products and services.

Times Online 100 Best Travel Sites
timesonline.co.uk/tol/system/topicRoot/100_best_websites/
Each year Times Online features its top 100 picks for online travel websites.
   The range varies from networking sites to vacation planning to specialty
   destinations.

Travelport
travelport.com
Travel distribution services and solutions.

Outsource Providers

All Freelance Work
allfreelancework.com

Elance
elance.com

GetAFreelancer
getafreelancer.com

Guru
guru.com

iFreelance
ifreelance.com

oDesk
odesk.com

Programming Bids
programmingbids.com

RentACoder
rentacoder.com

Publicity

The Publicity Hound
publicityhound.com

PRWeb
prweb.com

RSS Specifications
rss-specifications.com/rss-submission.htm

Search Engines

Ask
ask.com

Dogpile
dogpile.com

Google
google.com

Live Search
live.com

Search Engine Watch
searchenginewatch.com

Yahoo!
yahoo.com

SEO Tools and Resources

Google's Adwords External Keyword tool
adwords.google.com/select/KeywordToolExternal

Google Alerts
google.com/alerts

High Rankings
highrankings.com/seo-resources

KeyWord Discovery
keyworddiscovery.com

SEOBook.com's Keyword Tool
tools.seobook.com/keyword-tools/seobook/

Wordtracker's free keyword suggestion tool
freekeywords.wordtracker.com/

Yahoo! Search Marketing
sem.smallbusiness.yahoo.com/searchenginemarketing/

Social Networking and Online Communities

Digg
digg.com

Facebook
facebook.com

FlyerTalk
flyertalk.com

Google Groups
groups.google.com

GroupSense
groupsense.net

LinkedIn
linkedin.com

MySpace
myspace.com

Propeller
propeller.com

StumbleUpon
stumbleupon.com

Twitter
twitter.com

Yahoo Groups
groups.yahoo.com

Traffic Reports and Statistics

ClickZ Stats
clickz.com/stats
Net-related stats in a readable format.

comScore Media Metrix
comscore.com
Internet audience measurement service that reports on website usage.

eMarketer
emarketer.com
A great news source with an e-commerce focus and lots of stats.

Internet Traffic Report
internettrafficreport.com
Measures router volume at various points around the world.

Travel Websites

Chick Vacations
chickvacations.com

Expert Flyer
ExpertFlyer.com

Man Tripping
mantripping.com

Montrose Travel
montrosetravel.com

My Trip Journal
mytripjournal.com

New York Outdoors
newyorkoutdoors.wordpress.com

Our Cruise Planner
OurCruisePlanner.com

Pets on the Go™
petsonthego.com

Puppy Travel
puppytravel.com

Steele Luxury Travel
steeletravel.com

Viva Travels
vivatravels.com

Wanderlust and Lipstick
WanderlustandLipstick.com

Web Design and Site Tools

Bold Chat
boldchat.com
Online customer interaction software.

Bravenet
bravenet.com
Free tools and widgets.

CGI Resource Index
cgi.resourceindex.com
Free CGI scripts.

Direct Marketing Association
the-dma.org/privacy/creating.shtml
Privacy policy generator.

Download
download.com
Allows users to download trial versions and full versions of software.

FreePolls
freepolls.com
Free poll templates and widgets.

Free Scripts
freescripts.com
Free CGI scripts.

iWebTools
iwebtool.com/backlink_checker
Backlink checker.

Microsoft Publisher
office.microsoft.com/publisher/
Publishing software for designing websites, brochures, fliers, and newsletters.

100 Best Websites
100bestwebsites.org
Identifies 21 criteria it uses when selecting top sites.

osCommerce
oscommerce.com/
Open source e-commerce solutions

PC Magazine's Top 100 Websites
go.pcmag.com/topwebsites
Get inspiration for website design ideas.

Power Reviews
powerreviews.com
Customer reviews solutions.

Prospero Technologies
prospero.com
Social networking solutions.

Search Tools
searchtools.com
Search tools for websites.

Smart Guestbook
smartgb.com
Free guestbook.

Snipr
snipr.com
Reduces long URLs and tracks unique clicks.

Stock Photography
istockphoto.com
Royalty free photos and images.

SurveyMonkey
surveymonkey.com
Free poll templates and widgets.

TinyURL
tinyurl.com
Reduces long URLs.

Web Dev Tips
webdevtips.com/webdevtips/codegen/privacy.shtml
Privacy policy generator.

Web Developer
webdeveloper.com
One-stop shopping for advice and tools for building better websites.

Additional Resources

Successful Online Travel Entrepreneurs

Sue Freeman
Footprint Press, Inc. footprintpress.com
DisplayStands4You displaystands4you.com
NY Outdoors BLOG: newyorkoutdoors.wordpress.com

Dane Steele Green, President and CEO
Steele Luxury Travel
steeletravel.com

James and Heather Hills
Man Tripping
mantripping.com

Chick Vacations
chickvacations.com
MarketingHelpNet
marketinghelpnet.com

Chris Lopinto, co-founder
Expert Flyer
ExpertFlyer.com

Dan Parlow, CEO and co-founder
My Trip Journal
mytripjournal.com

Jenny Reed
Cruise Planners, Franchise Owner
OurCruisePlanner.com

Jennifer Sage, Owner
Viva Travels
vivatravels.com

Beth Whitman
Wanderlust and Lipstick
WanderlustandLipstick.com

Travel Industry and Marketing Experts

Al DiGuido, CEO
Zeta Interactive
zetainteractive.com

Peter Geisheker, CEO
The Geisheker Group, Inc.
geisheker.com

Andi McClure-Mysza
President of our Independent Contractor Division
Montrose Travel
montrosetravel.com

Jon Rognerud
E-business columnist for Entrepreneur.com and SEO consultant
jonrognerud.com

George Simpson
George H. Simpson Communications
georgesimpson.com

Associations and Organizations

Adventure Travel Trade Association (ATTA)
601 Union Street, 42nd Floor
Seattle, WA 98101
Phone: (360) 805-3131
adventuretravel.biz

Air Transport Association of America (ATA)
1301 Pennsylvania Ave., NW, #1100
Washington, DC 20004-1707
Phone: (202) 626-4000
air-transport.org

Airlines Reporting Corporation (ARC)
ARC Corporate Communications
1530 Wilson Blvd., #800
Arlington, VA 22209-2448
Phone: (703) 816-8525
arccorp.com

American Business Women's Association
9100 Ward Parkway
PO Box 8728
Kansas City, MO 64114-0728
Phone: (800) 228-0007
Fax: (816) 361-4991
abwa.org

American Marketing Association (AMA)
311 S. Wacker Drive, Suite 5800
Chicago, IL 60606
Phone: (800) AMA-1150 or (312) 542-9000
Fax: (312) 542-9001
marketingpower.com

American Society of Travel Agents (ASTA)
1101 King Street, #200
Alexandria, VA 22314
Phone: (800) 275-2782
astanet.com

Cruise Lines International Association (CLIA)
Florida Headquarters
910 SE 17th Street, Suite 400
Ft. Lauderdale, FL 33316
Phone: (754) 224-2200
cruising.org

Direct Marketing Association
1120 Avenue of the Americas
New York, NY 10036-6700
Phone: (212) 768-7277
Fax: (212) 302-6714
the-dma.org

International Airlines Travel Agency Network (IATAN)
800 Place Victoria, Suite 800
P.O. Box 113
Montreal, Quebec, Canada H4Z 1M1
Phone: (877) 734-2826
iatan.org

International Air Transport Association (IATA)
IATA Regional Office for the Americas
703 Waterford Way (NW 62nd Avenue), Suite 600

Miami, FL 33126
Phone: (305) 264-7772
Fax: (305) 264-8088
iata.org

International Gay & Lesbian Travel Association (IGLTA)
915 Middle River Drive, Suite 306
Fort Lauderdale, FL 33308
Phone: (954) 630-1637
Fax: (954) 630-1652
iglta.org

Merchant Risk Council
325 N 125th St., Ste. 300
Seattle, WA 98133
Phone: (206) 364-2789
Fax: (206) 367-1115
merchantriskcouncil.org

National Association of Commissioned Travel Agents (NACTA)
1101 King Street, Suite 200
Alexandria, VA 22314
Phone: (703) 739-6826
nacta.org

National Association of Cruise Oriented Agencies (NACOA)
7600 Red Road, Suite 126
Miami, FL 33143
Phone: (305) 663-5626
homebasedtrace.com/co-_op_nacoa.htm

National Business Travel Association (NBTA)
110 North Royal Street, 4th Floor
Alexandria, VA 22314
Phone: (703) 684-0836
Fax: (703) 684-0263
nbta.org

National Mail Order Association (NMOA)
2807 Polk Street, NE
Minneapolis, MN 55418-2954
Phone: (612) 788-1673
nmoa.org

Open Doors Organization
2551 N Clark Street, Suite 301
Chicago, IL 60614
Phone: (773) 388-8839
Fax: (413) 460-5995
opendoorsnfp.org

Outside Sales Support Network (OSSN)
22410 68th Avenue East,
Bradenton, FL 34211
Phone: (941) 322-9700
ossn.com

Professional Association of Travel Hosts (PATH)
pathonline.travel

Society for Accessible Travel and Hospital (SATH)
347 Fifth Ave, Suite 605
New York, NY 10016
Phone: (212) 447-7284
Fax: (212) 447-1928
sath.org

Travel and Tourism Research Association
ttra.com/

Travel Industry Association (TIA)
1100 New York Avenue, NW, Suite 450
Washington, DC 20005-3934
Phone: (202) 408-8422
Fax: (202) 408-1255
tia.org

Travel Publishers Association
PO Box 5346
Madison WI 53705
Phone: (888) 280-7060 or (608) 233-5488
Fax: (608) 233-0053
travelpubs.com

United States Tour Operators Association (USTOA)
342 Madison Ave., #1522
New York, NY 10173
Phone: (212) 599-6599
ustoa.com

World Tourism Organization (WTO)
unwto.org.

World Travel & Tourism Council (WTTC)
1-2 Queen Victoria Terrace
Sovereign Court
London E1W 3HA
United Kingdom
Phone: 44 (0) 870 727 9882
Fax: 44 (0) 870 728 9882
wttc.org

Government Agencies and Related Resources

The CAN-SPAM Act of 2003
ftc.gov/bcp/conline/pubs/buspubs/canspam.shtm

U.S. Census Bureau
census.gov

Department of Commerce
1401 Constitution Ave. NW
Washington, DC 20230
Phone: (202) 482-2000

Fax: (202) 482-5270
doc.gov

Department of Labor
200 Constitution Ave. NW, Rm. S-1004
Washington, DC 20210
Phone: (866) 487-2365 or (202) 219-6666
dol.gov

Internal Revenue Service
1111 Constitution Ave. NW
Washington, DC 20224
Phone: (202) 622-5000
irs.ustreas.gov

Library of Congress
Copyright Office
101 Independence Ave. SE
Washington, DC 20559-6000
Phone: (202) 707-3000
loc.gov/copyright

SCORE (national office)
409 Third St. SW, 6th Floor
Washington, DC 20024
Phone: (800) 634-0245
score.org

Small Business Administration
409 Third St. SW
Washington, DC 20416
Phone: (800) 827-5722
sba.gov

U.S. Business Advisor
division of the Small Business Administration
business.gov

U.S. Postal Service
usps.gov

General Small Business Resources

BizFilings
Information on incorporating and related services for business owners,
  including forms, advice, and tools needed.
8025 Excelsior Drive, Suite 200
Madison, WI 53717
Phone: (800) 981-7183 or (608) 827-5300
Fax: (608) 827-5501
bizfilings.com

BPlans.com
Free sample business plans, articles, and online tools.
144 E 14th Ave.
Eugene, OR 97401
Phone: (541) 683-6162
Fax: (541) 683-6250
bplans.com

Business Finance
Thousands of business loan and capital sources.
26741 Portola Parkway, Suite 437
Foothill Ranch, CA 92610
Phone: (866) 892-9295
businessfinance.com

Business Plan Center
Sample business plans and planning guidelines for business owners.
2013 Wells Branch Pkwy #206
Austin, TX 78728
Phone: (800) 423-1228
Fax: (512) 251-4401
businessplans.org

CCH Business Owner's Toolkit
Provides customizable interactive forms and spreadsheets, plus other business tools and resources.
toolkit.cch.com

Entrepreneur.com
Tons of resources, guides, tips, articles, and more at this informative website
for startup businesses and growing companies.
2445 McCabe Way, Ste. 400
Irvine, CA 92614
Phone: (949) 261-2325
entrepreneur.com

The Entrepreneur Institute
Provides resources and networking opportunities for business owners
3592 Corporate Drive, Suite 101
Columbus, OH 43231
Phone: (614) 895-1153
tei.net

Find Law for Small Business
Links to regulatory agencies, sample forms, and contracts, articles on all
aspects of business development.
610 Opperman Drive
Eagan, MN 55123
Phone: (651) 687-7000
Fax: (800) 392-6206
smallbusiness.findlaw.com

The Small Business Advisor
Lots of articles and advice for start-up businesses.
Box 579
Great Falls, VA 22066
Phone: (703) 450 7049
Fax: (925) 226 4865
isquare.com

Telecheck
Provides check-guarantee services.
5251 Westheimer
Houston, TX 77056
Phone: (800) TELE-CHECK
telecheck.com

Website Marketing Plan
Lots of informative articles, as well as sample business and marketing plans.
8050 Watson Road, Suite 315
St. Louis, MO 63119
websitemarketingplan.com

Franchise and Business Opportunities

The American Franchisee Association
53 West Jackson Boulevard, Suite 1157
Chicago, IL 60604
Phone: (312) 431-0545
Fax: (312) 431-1469
franchisee.org

BizBuySell
Useful website to find businesses for sale, as well as online tools and articles.
185 Berry Street, Suite 4000
San Francisco, CA 94107
Phone: (415) 284-4380
Fax: (415) 764-1622
bizbuysell.com

Cruise Planners
Phone: (888) 582-2150
cruiseplanners.com
beacruiseagent.com

Franchise Direct
Phone: (888) 712-1994 or (800) 719-0296
franchisedirect.com

Franchise Gator
599 W. Crossville Road
Roswell, GA 30075
Phone: (678) 748-3000
franchisegator.com

International Franchise Association
1350 New York Ave. NW, #900
Washington, DC 20005-4709
Phone: (202) 628-8000
Fax: (202) 628-0812
franchise.org

Trade Shows and Meetings

Specialty Trade Shows
3939 Hardie Road
Coconut Grove, FL 33133-6437
Phone: (305) 663-6635
Fax: (305) 661-8118
spectrade.com

Tradeshow Week
5700 Wilshire Blvd., #120
Los Angeles, CA 90036-5804
tradeshowweek.com

Tradeshow News Network
1904 Vintage Drive
Corinth, TX 76210
Phone: (972) 504-6358 or (972) 321-3705
tsnn.com

Books

The Entrepreneur's Almanac 2008–2009, Jacquelyn Lynn (Entrepreneur Press, 2007)

Home Based Travel Affiliate, Tom Ogg (Tom Ogg & Associates, 2007)

Open an Online Business in 10 Days, Melissa Campanelli (Entrepreneur Press, 2007)

Start Your Own Blogging Business, J.S. McDougall (Entrepreneur Press, 2007)

Start Your Own Travel Business and More, Rich Mintzer (Entrepreneur Press, 2007)

The Unofficial Guide to Starting a Business Online, 2nd Edition, Jason R. Rich (Wiley Publishing, 2006)

Publications and Magazines

Agent@Home
Published by Performance Media Group, LLC.
593 Rancocas Road
Westampton, NJ 08060
Phone: (856) 727-0035
Fax: (856) 727-0136
agentathome.com

Cruise Travel Magazine
Lakeside Publishing Company, LLC
990 Grove Street, Suite 400
Evanston, IL 60201-6510
Phone: (847) 491-6440
cruisetravelmag.com

JAXFAX Travel Marketing
52 West Main Street, Milford, CT 06460
Phone: (203) 301-0255
Fax: (203) 301-0250
jaxfax.com

Specialty Travel Index
PO Box 458
San Anselmo, CA 94979

Phone: (415) 455-1643 or (888) 624-4030
Fax: (415) 455-1648
specialtytravel.com

Target Marketing
1500 Spring Garden Street, 12th Floor
Philadelphia, PA 19130
Phone: (215) 238-5300
Fax: (215) 238-5270
targetmarketing.com

Travel Trade
22 E. 42nd street
New York, NY 10168
Phone: (212) 730-6600
Fax: (212) 730-7020
traveltrade.com

Travel Weekly
Northstar Travel Media LLC
100 Lighting Way
Secaucus, NJ 07094-3626
Phone: (201) 902-2000
travelweekly.com

Venture Travel Magazine
Kumuka Worldwide
45 Main Street, Ste. 309
Brooklyn, NY 11201
Phone: (800) 517-0867
Fax: (718) 923-0351

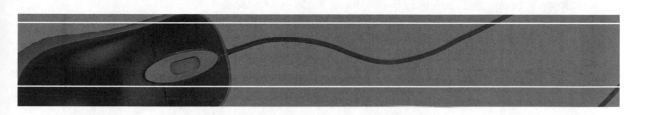

Glossary

Ad. For online purposes a web ad is a classified advertisement usually in the form of a banner, graphic image, or text image.

Ad impression. Occurs when a classified ad appears on a web page that is being viewed by a browser.

Adventure travel. Leisure vacations typically focusing on outdoor activities or cultural exploration.

Affiliate. A publisher or salesperson who sells a merchant's products or services through his or her own channels (i.e., website, newsletter, Google AdWords).

Affiliate directory. Categorized listing of affiliate programs.

Affiliate marketing. Revenue sharing between online merchants and website owners or online publishers.

Affiliate merchant. Advertiser or merchant in an affiliate marketing relationship.

Appointment. Designation to write airline or other travel product tickets.

Blogroll: A collection of links to other weblogs.

Booking: a travel reservation.

Click. When a browser/visitor interacts with a link or advertisement.

Community. A term used to identify a group of people who can chat on discussion forums, boards, and groups.

Concierge. Someone who performs special duties or requests on behalf of a client.

Digital certificate. An attachment to an electronic message used for security purposes.

Domain name. Textual name assigned to a website or business on the internet.

Drop-shipping. When a seller uses a wholesaler to ship auction items to winning bidders.

eBay stores. A venue for sellers to promote inventory through fixed-price listings.

Ecotour. Tour focusing on ecologically or environmentally sensitive areas.

Electronic file. A document prepared and stored in an electronic (as opposed to paper) format.

E-mail. Computer-based messages that are transmitted over telecommunication technology.

E-ticket. Electronic ticket issued by airlines instead of a paper ticket and boarding pass.

E-zine. An electronic magazine that is delivered through a website or e-mail newsletter.

Hard adventure tours. High-energy tour including athletic-oriented activities like white-water rafting or mountain biking.

Homebased travel agent. The rapidly growing segment of professional travel agents booking trips, including cruises and worldwide tours, from a home location.

Host agency. Travel agency (with appointments to write airfare, cruise, or other travel products) through which outside or independent agents sell products.

HTML. Stands for Hypertext Markup Language, a simple language used to create web pages; this language can be used to enhance eBay listings.

Impressions. The number of times an ad (text or banner) is viewed by a surfer.

Incoming or inbound link. Link from an outside site pointing to your site.

Independent travel agent. A travel agent who works alone or with a few associates or employees and is usually homebased.

Internet service provider (ISP). Any company that provides users with access to the internet.

Keyword. A word or phrase entered by a user when conducting an online search for something specific.

Merchant account. A special account with an acquiring bank that allows a merchant to accept credit cards over the internet.

Meta tags. Information used as tags to describe a specific web page that is visible to the search engines, but not site visitors.

Opt-in. Permission explicitly granted by recipient to receive a newsletter, e-mail, or other type of online correspondence.

Outbound link. Link pointing to another site from your site.

Password. A data string used to verify the identity of a user.

PayPal. Online payment service that allows merchants to accept credit card and bank account payments from buyers.

Products. Tours, cruises, hotels, and other elements sold by travel agents and tour operators.

Reciprocal link. Links exchanged between two sites.

RSS feed. A family of web feed formats, specified in XML and used for web syndication.

Search engine. An online program that indexes web pages and attempts to match them with users' search requests.

Search engine marketing (SEM). Promoting a website through a search engine.

Search engine optimization (SEO). Making a web page or site more visible to search engines to get a higher ranking.

Shopping cart. Software that interacts as an online business's catalog and ordering process.

Soft-adventure tours. Culturally oriented activities like antiquing or gardening.

Spam. Unsolicited commercial e-mail.

SSL. Acronym for secure sockets layer, aka digital certificate.

Text ad. Advertisement using text-based hyperlinks.

Tour operator or director. A representative who shepherds clients throughout tours.

Trackback. A mechanism for communication between blogs.

Travel supplier. Companies such as air and cruise lines, tour operators, and hotels that provide travel products.

Turnkey website. A site that has been fully developed for a specific product or service, which means the site has been designed, supplied, built, and installed to completion.

Uniform Resource Locator (URL). The complete address for websites, pages, or files on the internet.

Viral marketing. Marketing trend that encourages and facilitates people to forward and pass along marketing communications, such as putting affiliate links in a report or e-book.

Web browser. Software application that facilitates browsing of the internet.

Web design. Selection and coordination of available elements to create the layout and structure of a web page.

Web host. Stores your website, including graphics, and transmits it to the internet for other users to view.

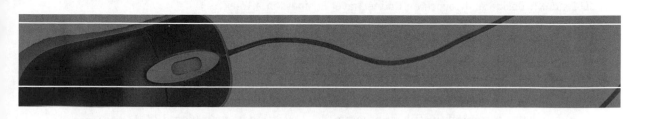

Index